Walks For All Ages
West Yorkshire

WALKS FOR ALL AGES

WEST YORKSHIRE

PAUL HANNON

BRADWELL
BOOKS

Published by Bradwell Books
9 Orgreave Close Sheffield S13 9NP
Email: books@bradwellbooks.co.uk

1st Edition

ISBN: 9781909914780

Print: Gomer Press, Llandysul, Ceredigion SA44 4JL

Design by: Andrew Caffrey. Typesetting by: Erik Siewko Creative

Photograph Credits: © Paul Hannon

Maps: Contain Ordnance Survey data
© Crown copyright and database right 2014

Ordnance Survey licence number 100039353

The information in this book has been produced in good faith and is intended as a general guide. Bradwell Books and its authors have made all reasonable efforts to ensure that the details are correct at the time of publication. Bradwell Books and the author cannot accept any responsibility for any changes that have taken place subsequent to the book being published. It is the responsibility of individuals undertaking any of the walks listed in this publication to exercise due care and consideration for the health and wellbeing of each other in the party. Particular care should be taken if you are inexperienced. The walks in this book are not especially strenuous but individuals taking part should ensure they are fit and able to complete the walk before setting off.

INTRODUCTION

It might well be claimed that there is no region in the land as diverse as West Yorkshire. Bounded to the north by the River Wharfe, to the east by the Plain of York, to the south by the Yorkshire coalfields, and to the west by the Pennine moors, this is a land of infinite variety.

The South Pennines form a high watershed that sends deep valleys eastwards to encounter large communities such as Huddersfield, Halifax, Keighley, Bradford, Leeds and Wakefield, together forming a buffer zone culminating in the arable landscapes of the east.

The Industrial Revolution saw the birth of the smoky mill town, as homespun textile industry in small villages was replaced by massive mills surrounded by rows of sturdy terraced houses to accommodate the new workforce. These larger Pennine settlements squeeze into a valley floor often shared with river, canal, road and railway. Steep flanks rise to those older villages, while higher still, rough pasture gives way to open moorland, where the mill chimney two miles away might as well be twenty miles distant. Many features of this district's industrial past provide interest to the observant walker. The hills are laced with a network of trading routes used mainly by packhorses: many of these stone causeways have laid dormant in wait for today's foot-traveller to bring them back to life.

Tumbling to the floor of the upper dales are short-lived but deep-cut and richly wooded little valleys known as cloughs, their fast-flowing streams harnessed for powering the flourishing textile mills. Up on the tops one is never far from a reservoir; the earlier ones made to serve the canals, others to slake the ever-growing thirsts of the towns. This is definitive gritstone country, and sharing the higher ground with the reservoirs are clusters of boulders and crags, these weathered natural outcrops outshining the countless sites of former quarries. Mainly small-scale operations known as delphs, these provided material for the drystone walls, reservoirs and buildings.

The area's principal rivers are the Aire and the Calder: the latter is entirely West Yorkshire's river, absorbing everything that its parent river misses. And despite the hilly nature of the Pennines, no fewer than four different canals are encountered on these walks. These feature the Five Rise Locks and Standedge Tunnel, two of the great wonders of the waterway age.

The northern fringe of the district features more affluent landscapes overlooking the Wharfe Valley, where Ilkley Moor and Otley Chevin gaze out into rural North Yorkshire. In the east of the region, meanwhile, fine mansions occupy elegant parkland at Harewood, Temple Newsam and Bretton Hall.

History, culture and scenery go hand-in-hand in these parts, fine examples being the World Heritage Site of Saltaire and the international literary (and landscape) attractions of the Bronte Country at Haworth. Victorian magnets such as the Cow & Calf Rocks, Hardcastle Crags and Shipley Glen still remain as popular today, joined by the likes of Summer Wine Country and the Yorkshire Sculpture Park.

HAWORTH

A RICH AND VARIED RAMBLE ONTO THE CELEBRATED BRONTE MOORS ON THE EDGE OF HAWORTH, ITS FAMOUS HEATHER CARPET JUST ONE OF MANY INTERESTING FEATURES.

Haworth ceased to be just another village when the fame of the Bronte sisters spread. The Focal point is the cobbled main street climbing steeply to the church of St Michael & All Angels, surrounded by pubs. Only its tower would be recognizable to the Brontes, the rest being rebuilt around 1880. Inside, the Bronte Vault holds the remains of all but Anne, whose grave overlooks the sea at Scarborough. Behind the church is the elegant Georgian parsonage of 1779, now a museum of its former occupants.

In 1820 Patrick Bronte had moved his family from Thornton near Bradford to the parsonage here. Though their brother Branwell had shown promise as an artist, it was the three sisters' brief literary careers that took off in 1847, when all three were published. Emily's solitary masterpiece, Wuthering Heights, encapsulates the mood of the wild landscape just beyond their very door, though sadly her and Anne's deaths rapidly followed the demise of Branwell in 1848. Charlotte's Jane Eyre was followed by further works, during which time she survived long enough to marry in 1854, though her flame was to burn out the following year. Patrick Bronte outlived all his children, attaining the ripe old age of 84.

Back down the main street is Haworth's second major attraction, the preserved Keighley & Worth Valley Railway. Although Haworth is at neither terminus, its station, with its locomotive works, is the hub of things. Haworth positively bristles with activity, with a range of special events including several based around the railway. It also has its own brass band and a particularly good information centre. Of numerous older buildings, the Old Hall dates from the 17th century, and is currently a hotel.

Penistone Hill is a tract of open country contiguous with Haworth Moor. The years have seen it change from man's workshop to his playground, with its former quarries now put to use as car parks. Grand views look north over the Worth Valley to the settlements of Oldfield, Pickles Hill and Oakworth, and back over Keighley to Rombalds Moor.

Bronte Bridge occupies the walk's turning point, a clapper-type bridge rebuilt in 1990 following flash floods.

By the path immediately before it is the seat-shaped stone known as the Bronte Chair, along with a 'psalm plaque' on a rock. Pushing the literary connection a little too far is the slender trickle known as Bronte Waterfall, in truth no different from a thousand other tinkling Pennine streams.

THE BASICS

Distance: 5 miles / 8km

Gradient: Minor uphill sections only

Severity: Moderate

Approx time to walk: 3 hrs

Stiles: Five

Maps: OS Landranger 103 (Blackburn & Burnley) and 104 (Leeds, Bradford & Harrogate); Explorer OL21 South Pennines

Path description: Good moorland paths, also field paths

Start point: Haworth main street (GR SE 029371)

Parking: Central car parks (BD22 8QR)

Dog friendly: Some sheep pastures, dogs preferably on leads

Public toilets: At start

Nearest food: Pubs and cafes at start, occasional tearoom at Drop Farm

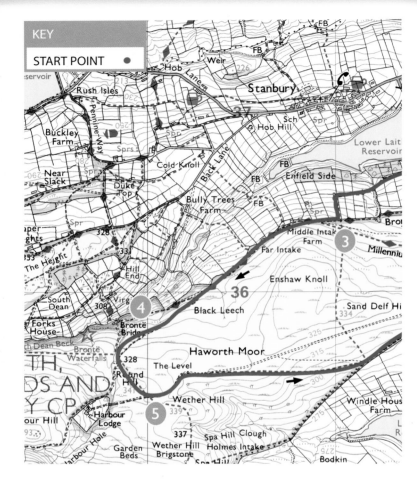

1. Facing the church at the top of Main Street, take a cobbled street just to the right, rising past the Kings Arms and churchyard to the Parsonage. Just past it an enclosed path takes over, emerging into open pastures. A splendid flagged path runs through fields to join West Lane. Just to the left fork left onto Penistone Hill, and ignoring an early branch left, keep straight on with super views over the Worth Valley. At a parking area opposite a cemetery take a broad track slanting down towards Lower Laithe Reservoir: off the moor it becomes enclosed above waterworks buildings and out onto a road by the dam.

2. Turn briefly left, and then take a small gate on the right. Cross a field bottom beneath Intake Farm to a gate/stile, then slant to a small gate at the top corner. Joining a walled

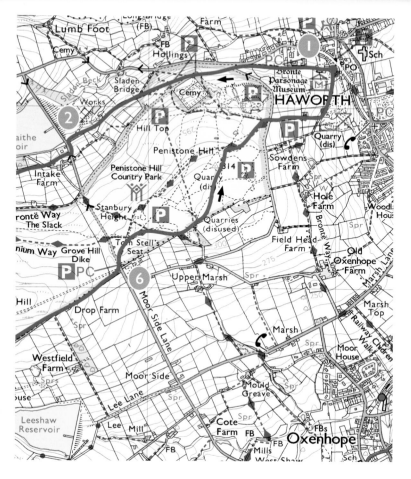

green way, go briefly right then leave by a gate on the left at a wood corner. A path runs outside the trees, then part enclosed, emerging and tapering to a stile into a field. Bear left across to a gate overlooking steps down to a side stream. Go up the other side, head away past a ruinous barn and along the left side of a crumbling wall to a barnyard. Turn left through gates and an old way ascends the wall side to a stile onto Haworth Moor.

3. Turn right on a firm track past a ruin, narrowing into a broad path as the moor opens out. The isolated farm of Harbour Lodge is seen ahead, while across to the right is the colourful side valley of South Dean Beck, into which you are about to descend. The rougher path runs down to arrive at Bronte Bridge.

4. Instead of crossing the bridge, leave by a lesser path climbing steeply up the right bank of the side stream boasting the Bronte Waterfall. This rough climb quickly levels out and the path runs gently on towards Harbour Lodge. Passing shooting butts the path runs to a small footbridge, just above which is the unsurfaced access road.

5. Turn left away from the farm, and on for some time until beyond an appreciable kink. After a slight rise as the road levels and straightens, it is seen for some distance ahead as it crosses the moor. However, a waymark sends a far more inviting path off right. With Leeshaw Reservoir ahead, this angles gently down to a wall along the bottom of the moor. A good path runs along to the left, joining Drop Farm tearoom's drive leading out to the road.

6. Rise left a short way, and before reaching Tom Stell's Seat on the brow, fork right on a stony access road onto Penistone Hill. Ideally using a parallel green path just to the right, rise to the brow of the hill, and a large car park. Just beyond it, at a wall corner, the track forks. Take the main, left one crossing to a cricket pavilion just ahead. A continuing path squeezes between a massive quarry hole on the left and cricket pitch on the right. Remain on the main path which angles away between hole and wall. Keeping left of further old quarries it curves left to a cross-paths at a modern sculpture, 'Literary Landscape'. Turn right to quickly reach a moor-edge road, across which descend the drive to Sowdens. Remain on the enclosed track continuing beneath it to a T-junction of ways. Take the path left, which runs firmly on to the church.

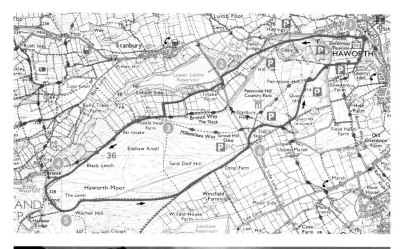

MIDGEHOLE

THIS WALK OF TWO HALVES COMBINES A NETWORK OF
PATHS THROUGH RENOWNED WOODLANDS WITH GENTLE
MOOR-EDGE TRACKS HIGH ABOVE CRIMSWORTH DEAN.
GRITSTONE OUTCROPS AND RICH WILDLIFE CAN BE FOUND
IN THE WOODS, AND FAR-REACHING VIEWS FROM ABOVE.

Hardcastle Crags is the name by which everyone
locally knows the valley of Hebden Dale, through
which flows the stream of Hebden Water. The
majority of this beautifully wooded, deep-cut
dale is in the care of the National Trust, and
draws crowds from far and wide. To witness
shy roe deer among the carpets of springtime
bluebells is a memory to treasure.

Alongside Hebden Water is the imposing Gibson
Mill, founded in 1800 as a water-powered cotton
mill. It ceased to operate in the 1890s, becoming
a surprisingly sited dance hall and even a roller-
skating rink during the mid-20th century – when
it was known as the Entertainment Emporium.
The well-preserved building is an impressive
sight in its wooded environs, and features a
cafe, shop and information centre, as well as
exhibitions and interactive displays. Now at the
forefront of sustainable 21st-century technology,
the National Trust are rightly proud that with no
National Grid connection, it produces its own
power by solar and water. Related features include a row of workers' cottages, while a
stone-arched bridge spans the beck. Around the back is a millpond.

Hardcastle Crags themselves sit just above the path beyond Gibson Mill. Taking the form
of a group of modest gritstone outcrops, they occupy a prominent knoll bedecked with
clumps of heather, with a slender ridge rising well above the treetops. As a result this airy
spot is a superb vantage point. Crimsworth Dean is a deep-cut valley that complements
the main valley of Hebden Dale. Running south from the high moorland of the Calder–Aire
watershed its lower section is deeply wooded in tandem with its neighbour.

THE BASICS

Distance: 4 miles / 6.4km

Gradient: One steady rise through woods

Severity: Easy walking

Approx time to walk: 2½ hrs

Stiles: None

Maps: OS Landranger 103 (Blackburn & Burnley); Explorer OL21 (South Pennines)

Path description: Good riverside and woodland paths and tracks

Start point: New Bridge, Midgehole, signposted off Keighley Road out of Hebden Bridge (GR SD 988291)

Parking: National Trust car park (HX7 7AL)

Dog friendly: Dogs preferably on leads

Public toilets: At start and Gibson Mill

Nearest food: Café at Gibson Mill

MIDGEHOLE WALK

1. From the bottom car park head up the drive a few strides until just past a solitary lodge, then fork left on a broad path slanting gently down to the lively stream of Hebden Water. Here a beck-side path is met, and this is accompanied upstream for almost a mile and a half to Gibson Mill, only straying from the bank to circumvent two short, impassable sections. The first impasse is very quickly reached as the path slants back up to the right a little to run a parallel course above the beck. At the fork, one drops back down to the beck to return a little later, or you could simply remain on this level one higher above the bank. Having merged, the path runs on to quickly drop back to the beck to commence a delectable stroll upstream, featuring characterful sections over tree roots and tightly by the water's edge. Further on, the path is forced slightly up again in two near parallel sections, to then run on again a little higher to soon reach a T-junction: drop left the short way to a clearing and a bench alongside stepping stones. From here an unbroken stroll leads upstream to the mill, passing further stepping stones. A 'psalm plaque' adorns a rock in the beck just before the final stepping stones as the mill appears ahead.

2. At Gibson Mill the drive is rejoined to climb above the beck, passing some fine carpets of bluebells. Levelling out twice alongside attractive clearings, the steep rise of Hardcastle Crags is seen up to the left, possibly inviting an ungainly scramble.

3. Continuing on from the crags, simply remain on the main drive. When a broad, lesser track branches left, your way swings uphill to merge with a firmer access road at the very top of the wood. The first open views reveal the Gorple moors to the left, up-dale, beyond the ancient hamlet of Walshaw with the impressive front of its shooting lodge.

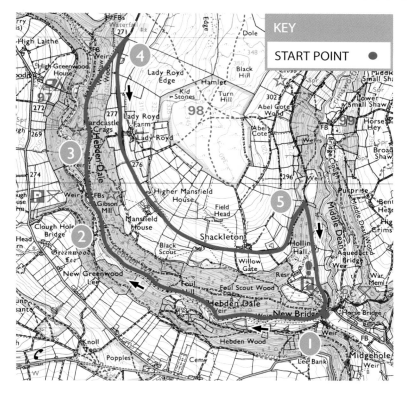

KEY

START POINT ●

4. Go right on this access road for a mile and a half of easy, level strolling to the hamlet of Shackleton, enjoying spacious open views over the wooded gulf of Hebden Dale below to Heptonstall Moor; ahead is Stoodley Pike. Remain on this access road which at the end drops left into trees and slants more roughly down to a junction.

5. Turn right here back into trees, ignoring any branches. Beyond an old quarry a firmer access road comes in alongside Hollin Hall, with further open views. Now surfaced for the final stage, trees are re-entered and the upper car park reached: unless parked here, take the near immediate path slanting left, which drops pleasantly down to the lower car park.

HEPTONSTALL

A SPLENDID AMBLE AS THE DELIGHTFULLY NAMED OPEN
COUNTRY OF POPPLES COMMON DIVIDES TWO DEEP,
WOODED VALLEYS, FREE OF ANY NOTICEABLE GRADIENTS.
GRITSTONE OUTCROPS AND BIG VIEWS FEATURE ALONG
WITH A CHARISMATIC OLD CLAPPER BRIDGE.

Heptonstall is a fascinating village that well merits a leisurely exploration. Steeped in history, it was of greater importance than Hebden Bridge until the arrival of the Industrial Revolution. Its exposed position, defended on three sides by precipitous slopes, has created a time warp in which its weather-beaten stone cottages revel. The Focal point is the churchyard which separates the imposing parish church of 1854 from the shell of the church of St Thomas à Becket, partly dating from the 13th century.

The poet/writer Sylvia Plath is buried here, as is 'King' David Hartley, leader of a notorious gang of 'coiners'. Hartley was executed in 1769 for his part in the murder of an excise man who had come too close to uncovering their practice of clipping and melting down coins and creating counterfeits. Alongside is the old grammar school of 1772, now a museum. Seek out also the octagonal Wesleyan chapel (1764), the old dungeon (1824) and the 16th-century Cloth Hall. There are two pubs, the Cross Inn and the White Lion, a post office/shop and a tearoom.

Hebble Hole Bridge is a 300-year-old clapper bridge consisting of two sets of great stone slabs in a charming location on Colden Water, part of an old traders' way linking Blackshaw Head and Heptonstall. The Pennine Way and Calderdale Way have one of their two meetings here.

Eaves Wood gives dramatic views from the crest of some alarmingly exposed gritstone outcrops, a point to bear in mind if small children are in the group. These good viewing platforms look down steep heather and bilberry-clad slopes into Colden Clough. Looking particularly grand is Stoodley Pike, seen at full height from the main valley floor to the towering moortop monument.

This was erected in 1815 to celebrate peace after victory over Napoleon, but later collapsed and was replaced by a new tower in 1856. It is upper Calderdale's most famous landmark.

THE BASICS

Distance: 3½ miles / 5.6km

Gradient: Mostly undulating, with only short uphill sections

Severity: Easy walking

Approx time to walk: 2½ hrs

Stiles: Eleven

Maps: OS Landranger 103 (Blackburn & Burnley); Explorer OL21 (South Pennines)

Path description: Good woodland and field paths

Start point: Heptonstall village centre (GR SD 987280)

Parking: Village car park (HX7 7NA)

Dog friendly: Sheep pastures, dogs preferably on leads

Public toilets: At start

Nearest food: Pubs at start

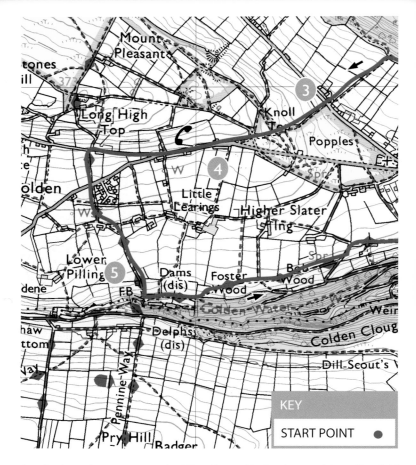

1. On the main street turn up the hill and beyond both pubs turn right on Townfield Lane. Continue past the last houses to a walled green lane which narrows to a footway. Emerging into a field, advance to the wall corner ahead, then bear left across two fields to a stile onto a road. Go briefly left to one opposite, and while a short path goes on towards a stile overlooking Hebden Dale, instead turn left on a thin field side path.

2. A largely level course immediately commences just above and then in the top of Hebden Wood for some time. A fork is reached fifty paces after a natural viewing platform: ignore that into the trees, and turn up an enclosed path, leaving at once by a stile on the right. Across a field the path resumes on the wood top, and then soon runs a little beneath the wall. Very soon, and before it begins a short descent

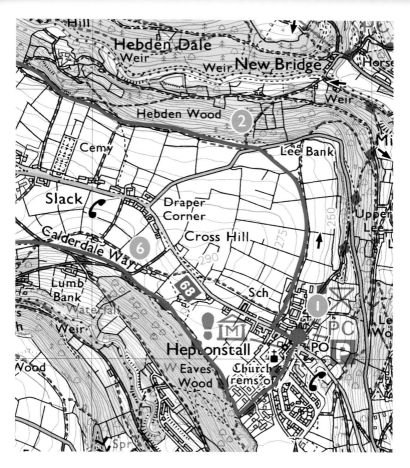

through the trees, look for a lesser fork left that runs the short way up to a corner wall-gap. Leaving the woods, an enclosed path rises away, and escapes at the top through a gap onto a drive at an old house, then joining a road just above.

3. Just a dozen paces on the right see a path rise onto a corner of Popples Common. Ascending thinly, on crossing a grassy track it becomes bolder and enters heathery surrounds. Walk along the right-hand wall and at the top rise to a path junction beneath a tall wall. Take the wall-side path left, keeping straight on across an access road and curving right on another track that slants

to the top corner of the common just ahead, emerging onto a road at Colden.

4. Turn right past rows of cottages to a fork, bearing right on Edge Lane. After a house on the left turn left down an enclosed path to rejoin the through road. Cross straight over and go down a driveway to a house. Go left through a small gate and then across to a stile/ gate in the wall below. A path slants down to the opposite corner of the enclosure, and from the stile/gate an enclosed, flagged path drops away. At the bottom it drops down to the edge of Colden Clough. Just below is a fork, and though your onward route is left on the flags, first take a minute's detour right down to Hebble Hole Bridge.

5. Retrace your steps to the fork and take that well-flagged path right, running beneath fields and above the drop to the beck. Entering Foster Wood a stile is met at a kink in the wall, and the stone causeway vacates the beck's environs to cross several fields, initially by slanting diagonally across the first one. When the flags end, the path becomes enclosed before merging with a similar way to rise to a junction with an access road. Go right, passing left of a lone house where a paved section leads to a spring before yet another enclosed path. Turn briefly down it,

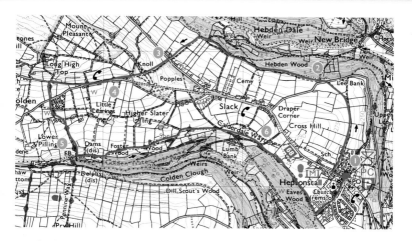

but keep left at a fork to run a level course onto a narrow access road.

6. Head up this a short way until a path strikes off right at a wall-gap into Eaves Wood. Keep to the upper, occasionally bouldery path for a grand level walk high above Colden Water. Soon opening out above Eaves Wood, the path remains with the left-hand wall until an enclosed path strikes left. To finish the walk keep straight on between houses to emerge by the church. Past here keep straight on past the old church to emerge onto the main street.

TODMORDEN

A WALK OF SUSTAINED INTEREST FROM AN INITIALLY STEEP CLIMB TO THE VERY MOOR TOPS OVERLOOKING A TYPICAL PENNINE MILL TOWN. ABANDONED FORMS OF COMMERCIAL TRANSPORT ARE LINKED, FROM HISTORIC PACKHORSE ROUTE TO CANAL TOWPATH.

Todmorden is a smashing little town with some outstanding buildings. Dobroyd Castle was built in the 1860s for the influential Fielden family, mill owners and local benefactors. The Town Hall was designed by their architect John Gibson in 1875, and features marble figures on a pediment above tall columns. The Old Hall was built in 1603 by the Ratcliffes, who long preceded the Fieldens in Todmorden circles: it has an intricate frontage of gables and mullioned and transomed windows. St Mary's Church is central but tucked away, while the more outgoing Unitarian Church of 1869 boasts a tall spire.

Unlike its counterparts, which thrived on the woollen industry, Todmorden and its mills were geared to the Lancashire cotton industry; indeed until little over a century ago Todmorden was literally on the border. Centre Vale Park features a fine statue of John Fielden, MP for Oldham: he was instrumental in the passing of an act in 1847 which meant women and children were saved from working more than ten hours per day!

While in the town you may spot evidence of Incredible Edible, an inspiring community project which campaigns for local food. From literally very small beginnings, local people began growing produce in nooks and crannies around the area, making valuable use of sometimes only tiny pockets of spare land.

The Rochdale Canal was completed in 1804, running 33 miles between Manchester and Sowerby Bridge. Its heyday was a brief one, and the demise began in 1841 when the Lancashire & Yorkshire Railway arrived. Today it is a colourful leisure facility with a succession of narrow locks bringing it down from its summit at the county boundary further south at Littleborough.

This section of the Pennines is criss-crossed by a network of old packhorse routes by which traders would lead their horses laden with all manner of goods from town to town and farm to farm. The Salter Rake was used for bringing salt across the Pennines from Cheshire, and like many others it features a well-preserved stone causeway – or causey – on which the pack ponies would find firm footing over less solid terrain.

Walsden occupies the deep valley bottom south of Todmorden, where its stream of Walsden Water joins the River Calder. Its countless rows of terraced houses and older cottages would have originally housed the local millworkers. On your entry into the village a more substantial house dated 1805 was the residence of Nobel prize-winning scientist Sir John Cockcroft (1897–1967), a pioneer in the development of peaceful uses of nuclear power.

THE BASICS

Distance: 3½ miles / 5.6km

Gradient: Sustained steep opening section

Severity: Easy walking after the steep start

Approx time to walk: 2½ to 3 hrs

Stiles: Three

Maps: OS Landranger 103 (Blackburn & Burnley); Explorer OL21 (South Pennines)

Path description: Steep lane, good moorland paths and towpath

Start point: Todmorden town centre (GR SD 936241)

Parking: Central car parks (OL14 7AA)

Dog friendly: Dogs preferably on leads

Public toilets: At start

Nearest food: Pubs and cafes at start, pub and fish shop at Walsden, pub at Gauxholme

TODMORDEN WALK

1. At the central roundabout outside the Town Hall head south on the Rochdale road. This is the short way to Fielden Square, bridging the Rochdale Canal en route. Cross the side road to Bankside, leading to Honey Hole Road. Rising steeply away, it jinks beneath the Unitarian Church, climbs past the clustered houses of Honey Hole and then a sharp kink takes it above the rear of the churchyard. With a grassy centre it pulls steeply up to some cottages.

2. The unsurfaced continuation bears left, more gently now between walls. Ahead is the moorland skyline of Langfield Common. On the right you pass the walled enclosure of a Quaker burial ground. When the track turns sharp left, exactly as the monument on Stoodley Pike is revealed far across on the

left-hand skyline, instead rise up a short-lived enclosed path straight ahead, emerging via a stile into a field. Ascend the wall side to another onto a moorland road.

3. From a stile opposite, ascend a field side to a stile onto an enclosed path that rises round the left side of a lone house. At the other side it resumes as a stone causeway climbing to a gate onto the foot of open moorland. A grassy track rises gently right, with massive views over the moors surrounding Todmorden. Curving up to the left it rises unfailingly and delightfully onto a brow, with the walk's summit marked by a cairned path crossroads at Rake End. You have now joined the packhorse route of Salter Rake.

4. Turn right on Salter Rake, at once starting a gentle slant down the moor, with the stone flags soon returning as you look down on Walsden and its steep-sided valley. This grand stride ultimately enters walled confines at North Hollingworth. Joining a driveway at this little hamlet, advance briefly to a junction.

5. With a splendid white-walled old house in front, go right on the surfaced access road descending steeply to the valley. At the bottom it passes above an abandoned section of old road and doubles back down to the edge of Walsden. Passing the tall-spired church it runs on to meet the canal.

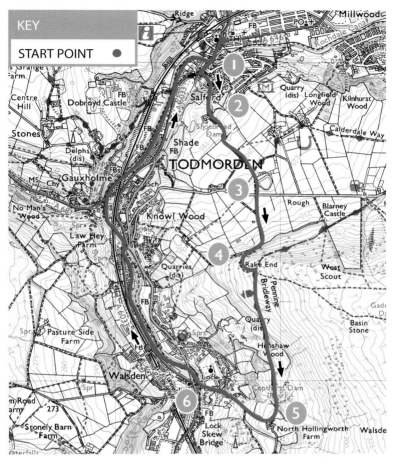

6. Across the canal turn right on its towpath, which is traced all the way back into Todmorden. Interest along the way includes a large number of locks, and the stream of Walsden Water running parallel for a spell: Walsden station and a fish shop are also handily placed in case of emergency. The only break of note comes when the main road intervenes: you must rise to cross both it and the canal before resuming on the opposite bank. An aqueduct carries the canal over the beck, and then you pass under a rail bridge alongside Gauxholme arches: the Masons Arms stands by Gauxholme Viaduct just a few strides off-route. Continuing under the Bacup road the railway soon crosses back above, and nearer the end an enormous brick wall opposite supports the railway. Here you curve round to rejoin the road on which you began alongside Library Lock, whose vertical bottom gate permits boats' access beneath the main road.

This walk undertakes an intimate exploration of the upper reaches of the Ryburn Valley from a characterful old village. The outward route shadows the course of the River Ryburn up to an attractive reservoir, returning along quiet roads and green lanes with open views.

Ripponden is a busy village, its old centre being a conservation area. Here the spire of St Bartholomew's Church reaches to the heavens, while alongside are a centuries-old

packhorse bridge and the white-walled and even more historic Old Bridge Inn. The railway arrived from Sowerby Bridge in 1881 and closed in 1958; sections of it are now put to use as footpaths.

The River Ryburn flows around seven miles from the high moors beneath Blackstone Edge to join the Calder at Sowerby Bridge. In the opening mile of the walk it provides delightful company embowered in woodland. Across it are several mills that have been transformed to residential use. A number of weirs testify to the traditional mill needs of times past, though the most action they see today is a heron taking flight.

During the ascent to Ryburn Reservoir you witness modern housing on the sites of textile mills. At the Ryburn Mill, a nice touch up until the 1990s was a quaint fire appliance in its own garage. Other surviving evidence is charmingly retained in the form of a number of millponds, supplied by weirs from the river and originally providing water to power the mills. Today they remain as valuable wildlife habitats encased in greenery.

Ryburn Reservoir was built in 1933 for Wakefield Corporation, and largely surrounded by woodland, and even with its hundred-foot-high dam it blends well in its deep fold of the valley. This is in contrast to its more recent and obtrusive neighbour Baitings Reservoir, whose massive concrete dam is visible higher up the valley. Baitings was completed as recently as 1956 on the site of a smaller reservoir.

The high-level return walk along Hollin Lane is an easy stroll with extensive good views over the Ryburn Valley to Norland Moor, and later down the dale to Sowerby Bridge. The fine early 17th-century houses of Beeston Hall, Great House and Low Cote are passed in this second half of the walk. Though all private habitations, there are good views of all of these splendid dark gritstone houses of differing stature.

THE BASICS

Distance: 4 miles / 6.4km

Gradient: Sustained steady rise to Ryburn Reservoir

Severity: Mostly easy

Approx time to walk: 2½ to 3 hrs

Stiles: Four

Maps: OS Landranger 104 (Leeds & Bradford) & 110 (Sheffield & Huddersfield); Explorer OL21 (South Pennines)

Path description: Good footpaths and lanes

Start point: Ripponden village centre (GR SE 040197)

Parking: Royd Lane car park just above the main road (HX6 4DH)

Dog friendly: Dogs preferably on leads

Public toilets: At start

Nearest food: Pubs and café at start, bar and sandwich bar at Slitheroe Bridge

RIPPONDEN WALK

1. From the church pass between the houses of Mill Fold and underneath the main road bridge over the Ryburn. A cobbled road heads upstream then passes through a small park onto a road. Advance along this by the river, and beyond houses and a small industrial estate a surfaced drive runs along the riverbank. When this ends at Ellis
Bottom Farm a path takes over to trace the Ryburn to a footbridge. Don't cross, but take a few steps up to resume through the trees. The path drops back to the Ryburn and on above a steep plunge to the river to reach a confluence. Just to the left the inflowing Booth Dean Beck leads you to a road, turning right to bridge the beck up onto the A672 at Slitheroe Bridge.

2. Use the main road to cross the Ryburn before departing left on Bar Lane, parallel with the river. This runs upstream to an eventual demise at new housing on the site of a mill. En route much housing is passed, then a millpond on the left and an almost hidden one on the right. A cobbled road takes over to climb to a hairpin bend. Here pass left of a garage in front, where a path is found with a millpond below and the dam of Ryburn Reservoir dramatically in front. Reaching a junction continue up, climbing steps to emerge at the dam end.

3. Don't cross the dam but rise right a few paces to a stile in a corner. A permissive path crosses the field to a stile into trees, and runs a lovely course soon giving better glimpses of the lake. Fields take over on the right as you reach Beeston Hall Rocks at the reservoir head. Just a little further is a path junction.

4. Pass through the first kissing gate but ignore the footbridge. Instead, take the ungainly path ascending the steep bank, quickly easing and fading to cross to a gap in the top right corner, with a big view of Baitings Dam. Ascend the wall side to a stile in the wall across the top. Over this turn right to enter Beeston Hall Farm past modern barns. Ignore the drive rising away and keep straight on towards a house ahead. As it swings right in front of it, the rear of Beeston Hall is just to your right. Your way now is the firm driveway heading left, quickly running out onto the A58.

5. Cross with care and head away along narrow Hollin Lane to the right behind a short terrace. This rises steadily for some time to an unsigned fork: take the initially cobbled Great House Lane rising left past a house, and almost levelling

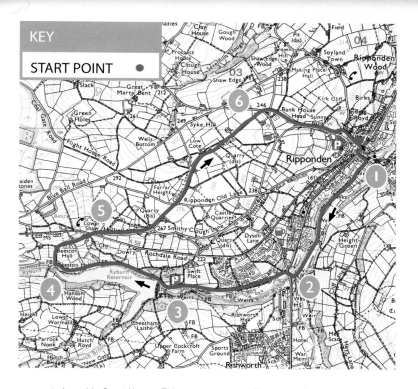

out alongside Great House. This runs on to meet Ripponden Old Lane. Go straight across onto Green Lane, a slight rise leading to the walk's summit marked by a seat. Just a short way further, where two bridleways come in from the left, take another one bearing right down a walled track. This is Cote Road, and on the left you pass the old house of Low Cote. Further, a firm driveway comes in to run on to another road.

6. Cross straight over behind a house, over a second road and along an enclosed cart track. Where it turns left just past a house, advance on over open ground. Down the wall side a narrow green path becomes tightly enclosed by walls to descend onto Royd Lane at a row of cottages. This leads steeply and rapidly down into Ripponden. If you wish to see the church cross straight over the main road down to the bridge and by the pub.

MARSDEN

THIS IS A MAGNIFICENT WALK THROUGH THE HEART OF THE
NATIONAL TRUST'S MARSDEN MOOR ESTATE, WHERE THE
UPPER REACHES OF THE COLNE VALLEY DRIVE A DEEP WEDGE
INTO MOORLAND.

Transport icons from another age include a packhorse bridge and a trans-Pennine canal and railway line that as the famous Standedge Tunnels burrow deep beneath the walk's dominant feature, Pule Hill.

Marsden is the first settlement in the Colne Valley, which runs an increasingly populated course down to Huddersfield. Large textile mills and terraced rows typify this once manufacturing-dominated town, and the valley was a hotbed of unrest when the Luddite movement was in full ferment. Near the stocks outside St Bartholomew's Church is the tomb of machine-maker Enoch Taylor; those who feared that his machines would take their jobs famously gave the name 'Enoch's Hammer' to the tools they used to smash them.

The Huddersfield Narrow Canal was built to convey goods between towns on either side of the Pennines, a twenty-mile route linking with canals at Huddersfield and Dukinfield. The impasse of Standedge demanded the construction of the highest, deepest and (at more than three miles) longest canal tunnel in the land. Until the tunnel's opening in 1811, goods had to be unloaded and carried over Standedge, a route still taken upon completion by the canal horses while the boatmen 'legged' their way through the tunnel by working their feet along the canal walls. Railway competition soon hit hard, though it wasn't until 1944 that the tunnel finally closed. Fast forward 30 years, and with just six locks remaining open, enthusiasts began a remarkable restoration programme that culminated at the start of the 21st century in the re-opening of Standedge Tunnel.

Tunnel End is a major focal point of the canal, featuring the Standedge Tunnel Visitor Centre in a canal warehouse, and a café at the entrance to the tunnel. Boat trips are available, from short forays into the tunnel to full-length journeys. Alongside, the railway also enters its own tunnel.

Close Gate Bridge is an outstanding packhorse bridge overlooking a lovely confluence. It is better known as Eastergate Bridge, a corruption of Esther's Gate, named after the landlady of a nearby inn. Bypassing Marsden to the south, Mount Road was the main turnpike route across Standedge prior to the building of the present A62 north of Pule Hill in 1839. As its name suggests, Old Mount Road was an earlier turnpike route, created by the celebrated Blind Jack of Knaresborough on the line of a packhorse trail.

THE BASICS

Distance: 4 miles / 6.4km
Gradient: Short steep pull from bridge to A62, longer very steady rise under Pule Hill
Severity: Moderate
Approx time to walk: 2½ to 3 hours
Stiles: Two
Maps: OS Landranger 110 (Sheffield & Huddersfield); Explorer OL21 (South Pennines)
Path description: Very varied: towpath, moorland and fields
Start point: Marsden parish church (GR SE 047116)
Parking: Roadside parking (HD7 6DG)
Dog friendly: Sheep pastures, dogs preferably on leads
Public toilets: At start
Nearest food: Pubs and cafes at start, pub and café at Tunnel End

MARSDEN WALK

1. From the church ascend the road to the railway station, and at the entrance take a gate on the left to join the canal at a lock. Go left on the towpath, a pleasant amble opposite heathery banks before passing under railway bridges to arrive at the old basin, watched over by a visitor centre. The towpath rises to a bridge at Tunnel End.

2. Cross the bridge and take a thin path slanting up the open green at the right end of a small parking area. Go through a gateway, cross an access road to rise right to the former Tunnel End Reservoir. Bear right on the firm path running left between reservoir and road. At the far end the beck is followed a short way before being ushered through a gate onto Waters Road. Go left past a terrace and a former generator house at Hey Green. At a bridge on the left, advance just a short way further up Blake Lea Lane, then escape left at an enclosed bridleway. This remains near the beck to run around to Close Gate Bridge.

3. Across the bridge, forego the path upstream, and go left the few strides to a ford on Redbrook Clough. Ideally advance a little further upstream to where solid slabs make crossing much easier. On the other side a small gate sends a steep path climbing between high walls, easing out to emerge onto the A62. Turn right on the footway and at the first house opposite, cross with care and take a stile to ascend a narrow enclosure on the near side of Moorlands Farm. At the top a small gate puts you onto the grassy moorland of Pule Hill.

4. Turn right on a thin path alongside the intake wall, passing the rear of this and a second house before commencing a gentle slant across the moor, parallel with the road below. Through a stile in a wall and then a gateway in a crumbling wall, the path runs grandly on up to the base of a spoil heap and an air shaft. Crossing a path rising from a lay-by, keep straight on your thinner one to meet a broad slanting track just above a second, lower airshaft. Just past it is a ruinous engine house. Still rising, a minute further a second green way slants down, this an inclined tramway from the quarries above. The path continues through bracken above the Carriage House, levelling out to run on to meet Mount Road.

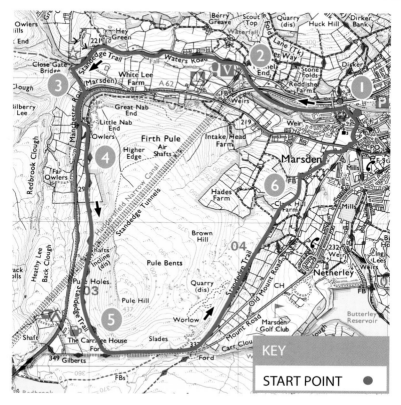

5. Turn left for two minutes to the brow, the summit of your walk, then gently declining as far as a junction with Old Mount Road. Go left here, and almost at once bear left along Hades Farm drive, which runs level for some time along the moor edge. Down below is Butterley Reservoir at the entrance to Wessenden. Ignoring two paths branching down to the right, keep on a little further; as a wall returns and the drive swings around to the left, advance the short way along the wall side down to a gate in a corner of the moor. Through it, a sunken way winds down between crumbling walls to Manor House Farm, its old house featuring mullioned windows.

6. Enter the confines at a gate and go left of the buildings to a gate at the bottom. Go down the side of the yard to a gate into a field. Descend alongside a deep-set hollow, winding down to a stile in the bottom into trees. Just below, a drive leads down to the right to Old Mount Road. Go briefly left to the A62, across which Towngate leads to the church.

DIGLEY RESERVOIR

This is easy walking around the headwaters of the River Holme amid a memorable blend of attractive reservoirs, colourful cloughs (side valleys) and old lanes. All this takes place in the dark shadow of Black Hill, best known for the road summit of Holme Moss that crosses its broad shoulders, occupied by an even better known radio (formerly television) mast some 750 feet (228m) high.

Digley Reservoir is a relatively modern addition to the water catchment of the upper Holme Valley, having arrived on the scene in 1952. The car park has been created in a landscaped quarry which provided stone for construction of the dam. Those seeking a much shorter stroll could opt to simply enjoy the reservoir circuit.

Holmbridge is based around the confluence of similar-sized valleys, those of Marsden Clough with the River Holme itself. Its centrepiece is St David's imposing church, with the Bridge Tavern well placed. Brownhill Reservoir dates from 1932, the youngest of four that occupy this part of the valley beneath brooding moors. Ramsden Reservoir (1892) is also seen, while Riding Wood (1883) and Yateholme (1878) are set a little further back.

Holme is a small but historic settlement nestled at the head of the Holme Valley, indeed set just within the Peak District National Park's northern boundary. Its attractive cottages include three-storey weavers' houses and a cobbled square. The Fleece Inn claims a steady passing trade on this infamous Woodhead Road climbing to Holme Moss. Entering the village you pass Holme Castle, a house with a castellated block dating from the 1820s, and opposite it a former school, still complete with its bell and inscription: 'Holme School rebuilt by subscription 1838': the date 1694 is carved on the door lintel. Note also a 1696 date stone on the arch at the small playground entrance in the village centre.

The dam of Bilberry Reservoir is a charming spot, looking across this smaller reservoir to the steep-walled and immensely colourful Marsden and Hey Cloughs. Bilberry Reservoir's engaging character belies its gruesome past, however, for this calm oasis was the scene of a major disaster in 1852.

Following a torrential cloudburst on the moors, its unstable twelve-year old dam burst and a swollen torrent raced down the valley to Holmfirth, taking 81 lives with it along with mills, houses and bridges.

THE BASICS

Distance: 3½ miles / 5.6km

Gradient: Minor uphill only

Severity: Mostly easy

Approx time to walk: 2½ to 3 hours

Stiles: Eight

Maps: OS Landranger 110 (Sheffield & Huddersfield); Explorer 288 (Bradford & Huddersfield) or OL1 (Peak District – Dark Peak)

Path description: Good field and reservoir paths and country lanes

Start point: Digley Quarry at the north side of Digley Reservoir, three-quarters of a mile off the A6024 at both Holme and Holmbridge (GR SE 110072)

Parking: Yorkshire Water car park (HD9 2RS)

Dog friendly: Sheep pastures, dogs preferably on leads

Public toilets: Holme

Nearest food: Pub and fish & chip shop at Holmbridge, pub at Holme

DIGLEY RESERVOIR WALK

1. From the car park don't rejoin the road, but
   cross to information panels and an enclosed
   path which will be your return route. Across
   it take a kissing gate, from where a path
   descends the heathery bank above the
   reservoir to rejoin the road. At once there are
   grand views over the reservoir to Black Hill.
   Continue the short way to a junction at the
   end of the dam. Don't cross, but continue
   down the road to a kissing gate on the right.
   The path briefly parallels the road before
   slanting down through trees to a kissing gate
   and steep steps onto an old road. Turn left on
   this through wooded surrounds for a traffic-
   free walk into Holmbridge, emerging past
   modern housing and a cricket field.

2. Turn right over the bridge and go left on a side road signed to Yate Holme. When
   it splits take the right branch, Bank Lane. Set into a wall on the left is a well
   dated 1834. The road becomes Brownhill Lane as it climbs to a junction. Keep
   straight on past several houses to reach the dam of Brownhill Reservoir, then
   on to approach Ramsden Reservoir. This section above Brownhill Reservoir has
   increasingly lovely views over its colourful banks to Black Hill.

3. Approaching the Ramsden dam, bear right down an enclosed path to cross the
   grassy dam just below its crest. Downstream is the head of Brownhill Reservoir. At
   the end the path slants up through trees away from the dam, ignoring two lesser
   branches left to gain a knoll on the spur between the arms of Brownhill Reservoir.
   It then curves round above the wooded bank until dropping to a footbridge on
   Rake Dike above a lovely waterfall. Slanting back up the other side the path levels
   out of the trees, then across a small pasture to adjacent stiles at the top corner
   above a wood. An enclosed path rises to a bridle-gate, then up the other side of
   the wall to a gate alongside a house set almost entirely below ground level. An
   enclosed cart track rises the short way onto the A6024 on the edge of Holme.

4. Turn left as far as the cobbled square, and then up through it and along the cul-
   de-sac Meal Hill Road. As the road bends left to rise towards the school, turn right
   through a gate and along a grassy walled way. When this expires contour across
   the field to a stile at the foot of the opposite wall, then continue above a wall,
   with Digley Reservoir appearing ahead. The waymarked path crosses a string

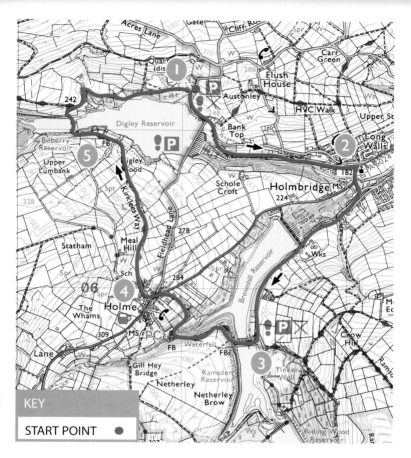

KEY

START POINT ●

of pastures linked by a mix of traditional and modern stiles. This grand stride remains reasonably clear, occasionally slanting right as Digley Reservoir becomes a major feature, aiming for its head. At the end the path drops right onto a broad path. Turn left on this through a bridle-gate, and rising away, it soon takes another in the adjacent wall into a colourful heather and bilberry tract near the reservoir. The path drops to the very head of the reservoir, which is also the embankment of Bilberry Reservoir.

5.   Across it a track slants away, doubling back right up to a junction of like tracks by a seat on open ground. Turn right to run on into trees, the way later narrowing to a footpath above the trees enclosing Digley Reservoir. It rejoins a track at the point where the old sunken way runs forlornly into the waters. This rises past a massive old quarry and on to the car park.

HOLMFIRTH

This simple and delightful walk demands some initial
effort to climb out of the valley, but features an
absorbing array of archetypal stone hamlets, wooded
cloughs, old field paths and lanes.

Holmfirth is the principal town of the Holme Valley in
its journey from Holme Moss to Huddersfield. It is a
characterful place whose nooks and crannies fully merit
a leisurely potter. The parish church of the Holy Trinity
replaced one damaged in a flood of 1777. Another
flood of 1944 caused three deaths, but by far the worst
disaster was the Bilberry Dam flood of 1852, in which
81 lives were lost along with mills, houses and bridges.
For decades Holmfirth was best known for saucy seaside
postcards, first produced by Bamforth & Co around
1910. Less well known is that Bamforths were pioneers
of silent films long before Hollywood became the place to
be! Since the early 1970s it has been the antics of a trio
of juvenile pensioners in TV's Last of the Summer Wine
that has kept Holmfirth on the map.

Though enlarged by modern housing, the lofty hilltop village of Upperthong is an old weaving
settlement, and a prominent reminder is the three-storey Weavers House on the main
street. Also along Towngate is the Royal Oak pub, outside of which a phone box has been
transformed into the village 'library'. Upperthong is also home to the Welly Wanging World
Championship, which takes place annually on the village's gala weekend. For the uninitiated,
to 'wang' something is to throw it!

At Hinchliffe Mill you pass a fine assortment of old houses, including three-storey weavers'
dwellings and a contrastingly squat single-storey terrace. The old goit runs alongside the
River Holme for some time before opening out into a splendid old millpond.

THE BASICS

Distance: 3¾ miles / 6km

Gradient: Sustained climb in opening mile, otherwise one further minor uphill

Severity: Quite demanding

Approx time to walk: 2½ to 3 hrs

Stiles: Eight

Maps: OS Landranger 110 (Sheffield & Huddersfield); Explorer 288 (Bradford & Huddersfield) and OL1 (Peak District – Dark Peak)

Path description: Varied paths and lanes

Start point: Holmfirth town centre (GR SE 141081)

Parking: Central car parks in Holmfirth (HD9 2JW)

Dog friendly: Sheep pastures, dogs preferably on leads

Public toilets: At start

Nearest food: Pubs and cafes at start, pubs at Upperthong and Hinchliffe Mill

HOLMFIRTH WALK

1. From the central junction of Victoria Street with the main road, go briefly left to the Information Centre. Just past it, before the library, turn up a path into the sloping Victoria Park. Stay on the main path which curves up right, and across a drive it rises to the top corner where a snicket runs out onto a road. Turn up this to the T-junction just ahead, and go right a few strides to a path squeezing between gardens. It winds steeply up through trees to run out between drives onto an access road at Hill.

2. Go left, leaving the houses behind as the enclosed cart track of Hill Lane takes over, rising ever upwards between fields. The track rises unfailingly to enter Upperthong at a sharp bend. Walk straight along the main street to a junction with Wickens Lane.

3. Bear left, down through a sharp bend out of the village. The upper Holme Valley opens out, dominated by Black Hill with its Holme Moss mast. Almost at once take a stile on the right, and cross the field centre to the next one. From there turn down the wall side to a stile onto a rough lane, and go right, dropping onto the A635. Cross and descend Black Sike Lane into Hart Holes Clough, and steeply up the other side to a junction, where you turn right: note the stone hut bearing an 1889 waterworks tablet. Just beyond, as the road opens out at Hogley Green, turn left on Hogley Lane, and keep left at an immediate fork to pass between houses and along to the old hamlet of Hogley.

4. Swing right between the buildings to a gate/stile out into a field. Walk across to the left side to a corner stile. From the next stile drop across the field centre to one opposite, then advance along the field-top to a stile onto a road. Go right to the lone house whose origin is etched above the door: 'This school built by subscription 1816'.

5. Just a few strides above it a grassy pathway turns down its far side, swinging pleasantly down between walls to a kissing gate before a sharp bend at a path junction. Ignore the

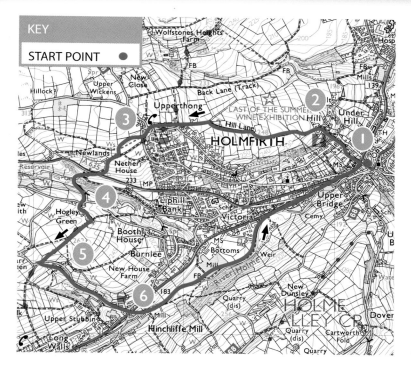

stile ahead and turn left down this inviting broad way to a gate/stile above a wooded clough. The path resumes splendidly above the edge of the clough to join a drive at Upper Stubbin. Don't follow this down, but cross straight over to a tiny path quickly emerging between houses into a field. A largely stone surfaced path descends to a stile at the bottom by Stubbin Farm, from where a driveway descends to the A6024 at Hinchliffe Mill.

6. Cross straight over and bear left along Old Road to an angled crossroads. At the end go straight ahead on Water Street past millworkers' cottages. At the road end keep straight on past the end of the mill to a footbridge on the River Holme. Don't cross, but head downstream on a path between the mill-race and river. This runs through wooded surrounds and out into a sizeable millpond backed by a mill at Burnlee. Towards the end of the pond, drop to a bridge on the river. Don't cross but resume downstream on a path squeezing between mill and river. Beyond the mill the enclosed path runs past a weir to reach new housing, where a short cobbled section leads up to the A6024. Turn right on the footway shadowing the main road back into town, the river soon departing at another millpond.

FARNLEY TYAS

An outstanding Iron Age hillfort crowned by a Victorian tower is the unmissable focal point of this delightful country walk above the village of Almondbury and high above the Holme Valley and the busy town of Huddersfield.

Farnley Tyas is a pleasant hilltop village looking across the tranquil Woodsome Valley to Castle Hill. At its heart are the church of St Lucius and the Golden Cock pub. A wooden seat near the start and finish of the walk makes a serene viewpoint for the route of this ramble, and is appropriately inscribed 'Majestic Castle stands proudly among the hills'.

The landmark of Castle Hill looms high above all its surroundings, its stature further enhanced by the imposing Victoria Tower completed in 1899 to commemorate Queen Victoria's Diamond Jubilee two years earlier. It is normally open on afternoons at school holidays and weekends, and for a fee you can climb the interior to escalate the already massive panorama. Enormous views in all directions are particularly impressive westwards, where the saddleback of Meltham Moor is distinctive as it fronts many miles of Pennine moorland skyline.

Despite evidence of Neolithic (New Stone Age) occupation perhaps 4,000 years ago, Castle Hill is better known for the Iron Age hillfort that existed here around 2,000 years later in an almost ready-made location. The extensive ditches and ramparts make for an excellent circuit around the perimeter, and were later incorporated into the defences of a motte and bailey castle built around 800 years ago by the de Lacy family. A well and some modest sections of wall survive. The castle became a hunting lodge before falling into ruin around 1320.

This obvious beacon site was first used to warn of the approach of the Spanish Armada in 1588, and a modern-day beacon is in place to celebrate noteworthy occasions.

Political and religious and social rallies took place here notably in the 19th century, along with what would today be deemed unsavoury 'sporting' events. A World War II anti-aircraft battery was also placed here. A pub first built in 1810 was replaced in 1852: the Castle Hill Hotel was sadly demolished in 2005 after planning violations, with plans for a replacement in a state of limbo.

THE BASICS

Distance: 3 miles / 4.8km

Gradient: One notable climb from Lumb Dike to Castle Hill

Severity: Moderate

Approx time to walk: 2 to 2½ hrs

Stiles: Thirteen

Maps: OS Landranger 110 (Sheffield & Huddersfield); Explorer 288 (Bradford & Huddersfield)

Path description: Mostly faint field paths

Start point: Farnley Tyas village centre (GR SE 164127)

Parking: Roadside parking (HD4 6UD)

Dog friendly: Dogs preferably on leads

Public toilets: None

Nearest food: Pub at start

FARNLEY TYAS WALK

1. Facing the pub, turn right and immediately left at the road junction. Turn down an enclosed cart track after the first house. This drops away and swings sharp left to end at a bench with lovely views across to Castle Hill. Through the gate turn right down the field side to a gate/stile part way down. A cart track descends Royd House Wood, crossing a small stream. The path shortly emerges from the trees. Almost immediately re-entering woodland, it runs a short, level course to leave the trees at the other side. Go to the right of the boundary wall and along a path shadowing it down to a stile at the end. A path heads away through scattered trees, descending steps into Lumb Dike.

2. A bridge crosses the stream and the path ascends the other side to a stile. Ascend the field with the hedge on your left, through a gateway and up a second field side to a stile at the top alongside a house at The Lumb.

3. Joining Lumb Lane turn briefly right to a stile on the left. A steep field-side climb leads to a gap at the top, then up again to a stile onto a rough access road. Just to your left another stile resumes your climb, becoming enclosed in greenery and slanting left into colourful undergrowth. At the rear of a hidden house a signed path doubles back right, up out of the undergrowth to emerge alongside a fence with open views. Immediately above you is the outer bank of Castle Hill fort. Follow the path right with the fence to emerge onto the end of the site, rising to meet a firm path encircling the outer bank. You can now follow this back around the other side of the fort, or at a cross-paths you can ascend to follow the bank top. Either way will take you to the Victoria Tower.

4. Leave by a hard path running a few strides from the tower to steps descending onto a road. Go right to a T-junction, then left with a footway. Immediately before the second house on the left take a stile set back across the yard. Follow a wall away. At a kink in it go sharp right across the field centre to an outer corner, and through the gateway turn left to resume along the wall. Through an intervening stile this leads to a stile in the bottom wall. Turn sharp right to a gate/stile above Roaf Wood, and on again through a corner stile ahead, leaving the wood edge to rise with an old wall on

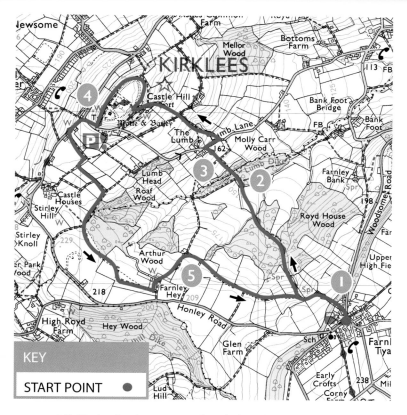

KEY

START POINT ●

your left. At a bend part way up pass through the wall and a clear path crosses an extensive sloping field. This runs a near-level course through two scant lines of old trees and on to the far end where a gap puts you onto an access road.

5.   Go left past the cottages at Farnley Hey, and at the end go right to find an enclosed path descending into a field. Slant right to a stile in the descending wall, then down the field side to a stile onto a path junction in front of a modern guide stone. Bear right along a short-lived enclosed path, and at the end cross a track to a stile. Your path then crosses another sloping pasture, meeting an outer boundary corner to lead to the far end. Here is another path junction: go straight ahead for a few enclosed strides into a field, and resume along several field bottoms. At the end slant gently above a line of old trees to rejoin the outward route at the start of the enclosed way, which you follow back up into the village.

WEST BRETTON

Sitting next to a junction of the M1 motorway on the edge of the village of West Bretton, Bretton Country Park is a thoroughly absorbing location for the Yorkshire Sculpture Park, with a regularly changing display of outdoor exhibits. As most of these are temporary, few can be used in the route description as they are likely to have been replaced when you come this way!

The Yorkshire Sculpture Park is open from 10am to 6pm all year except Christmas Eve and Christmas Day. Entry is free, but there is an appreciable parking charge. The park opened to the public in 1977, and from modest beginnings an area of some 500 acres can now be explored to discover what is effectively a quite amazing outdoor gallery. Works by local 'superstars' Henry Moore and Barbara Hepworth feature amid a fascinating, ever-changing range of sculptures.

The first documented house on the site was built for Sir Thomas Wentworth, Knight Marshall to Henry VIII. Damaged by fire in 1720, it was replaced by the present Hall in the 1730s for Sir William Wentworth. For around half a century until 1977, the house and ancillary buildings formed a campus of Leeds University, which after several derelict years is likely to be transformed into a hotel in the near future.

In the 1760s Sir Thomas Wentworth Blackett set about landscaping the park, and the husband of his illegitimate daughter Diana, Colonel Thomas Richard Beaumont, carried out major landscaping work between 1792 and 1831. Numerous ornamental Romantic structures were spread around the grounds, of which the following are all passed on the walk. The Camellia Plant House dates from around 1812; the Summer House is an early 19th-century folly built to echo the architectural style of a Greek temple, and it occupies a commanding position overlooking the Upper Lake; the Obelisk was possibly erected to show the site of the former Bretton Hall; the late 18th-century Shell Grotto retains old shells affixed to its interior.

The boathouse features six stone columns surviving from the original building, dating possibly from as far back as the 1760s: it now stands landlocked in woodland due to silting up. The old canal known as The Cut was created to carry water from the River Dearne past the lakes to supply a blast furnace within the park. St Bartholomew's Chapel was designed by Sir William Wentworth in 1744, and now houses small exhibitions.

THE BASICS

Distance: 2 miles / 3.5km

Gradient: Negligible

Severity: Very easy

Approx time to walk: 1½ to 2 hrs

Stiles: None

Maps: OS Landranger 110 (Sheffield & Huddersfield); Explorer 278 (Sheffield & Barnsley)

Path description: Very easy, mostly firm parkland paths

Start point: Yorkshire Sculpture Park visitor centre (GR SE 286131)

Parking: Main car park at Yorkshire Sculpture Park (charges apply) (WF4 4JU)

Dog friendly: Dogs on leads. No dogs permitted in Upper Lake section (which can be omitted)

Public toilets: At start and Rushbond Building

Nearest food: Café at start and Rushbond Building

WEST BRETTON WALK

1. At the Visitor Centre, pass through and out along the western exit into the formal garden. Drop down solid steps immediately in front to the entrance to the Underground Gallery. Turn left through a big hedge gap then sharp right along a terrace to emerge on the edge of open parkland. Cross the access road in front then drop left on the grass, passing a pond, and continue further down the grass to the Rushbond Building (YSP Learning, formerly the Kennel Block).

2. Continue straight down into 'Arcadia', in the Lower Park, passing more exhibits to reach a large open court with an enormous 'rabbit' sculpture – 'Sitting' – at the far corner outside the Camellia House. Continue down the grass again and a path drops onto a broader pathway, with the Lower Lake in view ahead. Turn right along this to quickly arrive at a cross-paths with a broad access track. Just to your left is a bridge over the canal, with Cascade Bridge, crossed later in the walk, immediately beyond it.

3. For now go straight to a gate into the wooded surrounds of the Upper Lake. A broad track heads away, while the more interesting right branch path rises slightly though the trees to pass the Summer House and drops down past the Obelisk to rejoin the main way. This curves around to bridge the broad canal to the boathouse and over the very head of the lake before swinging left to return down the south bank. A footbridge crosses a small ravine. A bird hide sits just to the left. Where the path forks, the left option visits the Shell Grotto and gives further good views over the lake. They rejoin and emerge onto the access road just above Cascade Bridge.

4. Go left to cross Cascade Bridge this time, then immediately right through a gate to head along the shore of the Lower Lake. This offers a grand stroll past further sculptures and just beneath the canal whose own path makes it a great foreground

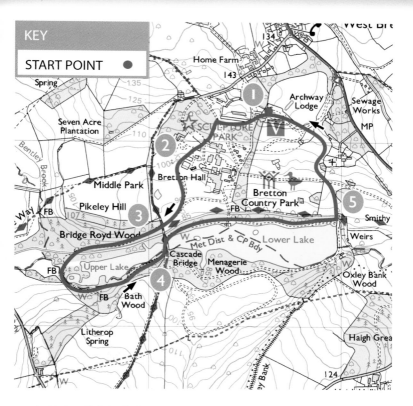

KEY

START POINT ●

to Bretton Hall itself. Shortly you merge into a stony access road alongside a boathouse, with a bridge to the left. Keep on this lakeshore track to arrive at the far end alongside the dam. Turn left up the path to bridge the canal as it turns to drop through cascades, and through a gate you enter the open parkland.

5. A lovely grassy path rises away, slanting left a little to pass through a gate on a stony access road alongside stone walled sheepfolds. Up above is a Henry Moore sculpture. Now bear right to a path in trees accessing the tree-shrouded chapel. Re-emerging, big open views look over the park to the high Pennines far beyond, along with the upper section of Emley Moor TV mast. The access track can be quickly left for a firm grass path slanting right, making its way back to the waiting visitor centre, possibly by way of another Henry Moore sculpture up to the right.

WINTERSETT

Effortless walking explores varied scenery to the south of Wakefield, where old coal mining sites have been replaced by peaceful leisure facilities. Reservoir, woodland and canal towpath feature in this stroll that also witnesses the site of the country's first, unofficial, enterprised nature reserve.

Anglers Country Park occupies a former coal mining site, said to have at one time been the country's deepest open-cast mine at a depth of some 250 feet. The mine closed in 1982, and before long the rather soulless yet nevertheless soothing lake was sitting amid a reinvigorated landscape. Be aware that local information that its encircling path is two miles (3km) in length is massively exaggerated. The lake is especially popular with waterfowl arriving to spend the winter here. The popular visitor centre (with tearoom and WCs) is closed on Mondays.

In the 1600s Haw Park Wood was part of the ancient Don Forest that was largely felled to make way for agriculture. The mid-20th century saw much ancient woodland replanted in order to produce timber and pit props for the local coal mining industry, but the wood is now being gradually returned to a deciduous scene from its pines and larches.

The Barnsley Canal was completed in 1802, principally to carry coal north from Barnsley. It ran roughly 15 miles to Heath Common on the outskirts of Wakefield, where it linked with the mighty Aire & Calder Navigation. It was abandoned in 1947 and closed in 1953 after a major leak had flooded a housing estate. Only limited sections still carry water, but there are long-term plans to restore this historic waterway. Wintersett Reservoir was built in 1793 to supply the canal, and was enlarged in 1807. Cold Hiendley Reservoir was built with a similar purpose in 1854 and enlarged 20 years later.

The walk spends some time alongside a monumental three-mile-long stone wall built by Charles Waterton (1782–1865). Known locally as 'Squire' Waterton, this pioneering Victorian naturalist brought species back from the tropical forests of South America, and in 1813 created what was looked upon as the world's first nature reserve.

Dating from 1767, his home Walton Hall occupies an island on a lake, and is now the Waterton Park Hotel. The great wall helped protect and contain the wildlife, while the Watch Tower you visit was just one of six from where he could watch over his estate and animals. Dating from around 1820, it was restored in 2005.

THE BASICS

Distance: 4¼ miles / 6.8km or 3 miles / 4.8km
Gradient: Virtually level
Severity: Very easy
Approx time to walk: 2½ hrs
Stiles: None
Maps: OS Landranger 110 (Sheffield & Huddersfield) or 111 (Sheffield & Doncaster); Explorer 278 (Sheffield & Barnsley)
Path description: Mostly firm paths
Start point: Anglers Country Park (GR SE 375153)
Parking: Car park at Anglers Country Park and The Heronry Waterton Countryside Discovery Centre, signed along Haw Park Lane (WF4 2EE)
Dog friendly: Dogs preferably on leads
Public toilets: At start
Nearest food: Café at start, pub in village

WINTERSETT WALK

1. From the car park rejoin Haw Park Lane and turn right. Remain on this all the way to losing its surface as it trades woodland for ploughed fields to approach Haw Park Wood. Within a minute of entering, a major junction is reached. The way ahead is your return route, so for now turn sharp left along a firm woodland track. At the fork keep left to run along the wood edge, soon swinging right to drop gently through the trees alongside a replanted area. When the track swings sharp right at the bottom, continue straight down a less firm, still broad path. Stone steps on your left lead down to Fox's Well, while the path continues to a corner junction in front of the drained Barnsley Canal.

2. Turn left to leave the wood corner, and advance a few strides over the bridge of the outflow of Cold Hiendley Reservoir to appraise its attractive scene. Re-entering the wood, ignore a firm cycle track bearing immediately left, and instead continue just a few strides further onto a thinner but clear path on the near side of the canal. This runs a delightful course through the wood on a slight bank. An early stone-arched bridge is passed before the canal becomes part watery. Maintain this route until nearing the wood corner, meeting a broader path from the right to approach Clay Royd Bridge.

3. This time cross the bridge to a path crossroads, and turn right to finally join the canal side track. This runs for some time along the bank, with open fields to your left. Passing beneath a tall-arched bridge in a deep cutting, remain on the towpath a little further until a firm path doubles sharply back to slant up to an access road.

4. Turn left over the bridge and along this road which swings sharp right between estate wall and canal. Turn left off this broad way on a footpath outside the estate wall. Stay on this path as it descends gently to re-enter Haw Park Wood. The path broadens as it climbs through the trees, a near dead-straight course still with the wall. On easing out it runs on to where the wall departs left.

5. A kissing gate in the wall permits a 300-yard detour on a delightful path between wood and golf course to Squire Waterton's Watch Tower. Back at the gate, your path

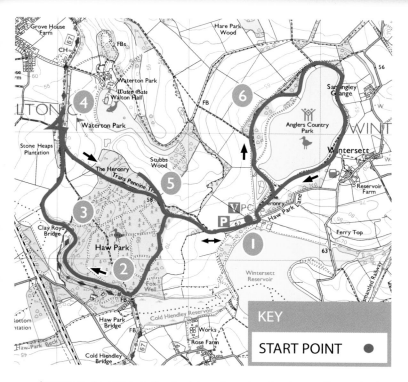

KEY

START POINT ●

resumes to rise slightly further to pick up the outward route near the wood edge. Advance straight on this, back out of the wood, to return along the lane to the car park.

6. For the part two option, pass through the gates at the rear of the car park to the visitor centre. This section is a very simple loop encircling Anglers Country Park reservoir, which appears ahead. Keep to the left path along a hedge side, passing a bird hide to approach the reservoir. Keep left at a fork before it, passing Pol Hide at a pond just to the left, and on away from the reservoir. An early right branch gives quick access to the main bird hide overlooking the reservoir, and a short-cut return path puts you back on the main route. Now simply remain on its negligibly rising course enclosed in greenery. After levelling out a right branch takes you into a grassy area by the shore, and a little further the other branch comes back in. All is now entirely open as the firm path leads all the way back to the visitor centre. Near the end, a signposted path offers a short diversion left into Wintersett village to visit the Anglers Retreat pub.

TEMPLE NEWSAM

Easy walking leads around numerous interesting features set within a great estate on the very outer limits of a great northern city.

Temple Newsam is an imposing Jacobean mansion set within beautiful, well-wooded parkland. Its origins date back to a preceptory of the Knights Templar, medieval mercenaries. Its predecessor was the birthplace in 1545 of Lord Darnley, husband of Mary, Queen of Scots. Most of the enormous red-brick house dates from the 1630s:

for 300 years it was home to the Ingrams until acquired by Leeds Corporation in 1922. Its remarkable array of contents displayed within around thirty rooms includes a nationally important art collection. Externally its south front looks out over charming hedged gardens, while set around the 1788 skyline balustrades of its eastern courtyard are the following words: ALL GLORY AND PRAISE BE GIVEN TO GOD THE FATHER THE SON AND HOLY GHOST ON HIGH PEACE EARTH GOOD WILL TOWARDS MEN HONOUR TRUE ALLEGIANCE TO OUR GRACIOUS KING LOVING AFFECTION AMONGST HIS SUBJECTS HEALTH AND PLENTY BE WITHIN THIS HOUSE.

To the east of the house an 18th-century stable block houses a visitor centre, exhibition rooms, estate shop, tearoom and WCs. Adjacent Home Farm has been transformed with a hugely successful rare breeds programme featuring hundreds of cattle, sheep, goats and pigs, and also has a 300-year old Great Barn. Set just above the lower lakes is the beautiful red-brick Walled Garden, at the centre of which is an extensive rose garden. Both the house and the farm have entry fees, but only the car park adjacent to the house has parking charges.

The rolling parkland was designed by Capability Brown in the 1760s, and offers extensive, relaxing walking opportunities. Awaiting restoration, the Little Temple occupies a knoll with a view over encroaching undergrowth to the house. Encountered on the walk at the eastern boundary of the grounds is the linear earthwork of Grime's Dyke (or Grim's Ditch). Of uncertain origin, it may date from Roman times, or was possibly a later British defence of the kingdom of Elmet (Elmete). A contrastingly modern boundary is effectively drawn by the great curving sweep of the M1 motorway, which skirts the edge of the parkland.

The fringes of the grounds were exploited for coal until quite recent times. Just outside the grounds at the road entrance is the lovely St Mary's Church at Whitkirk, containing some fine effigies.

THE BASICS

Distance: 2¾ miles / 4.5km

Gradient: One notable rise to The Avenue

Severity: Easy

Approx time to walk: 2 hrs

Stiles: Four

Maps: OS Landranger 104 (Leeds & Bradford); Explorer 289 (Leeds)

Path description: Good estate paths and tracks

Start point: Temple Newsam, signed along Colton Road off the A63 at Whitkirk (GR SE 358321)

Parking: Several car parks (LS15 0AE)

Dog friendly: Dogs on leads in Walled Garden

Public toilets: At start and at Walled Garden

Nearest food: Cafe at start

1. From the house follow the firm path with the front garden on your right. At the end the broad path advances slightly left to a crossroads of ways, where you cross straight over to curve down to the left, emerging from greenery with open views over the M1. At the bottom it merges with a level, solid way from the right. Go left, and a short way further, through a gate, is a junction of ways.

2. Double back right on this, dropping to cross a tiny stream and swinging left to another three-way junction. Turn right here; the track rises away between trees and soon swings left for a sustained climb between hedgerowed pastures. On the brow it finally levels out with big views, including glimpses back to the mansion. The continuation runs left to terminate at a gate fronting two large pastures surrounded by woodland. From a stile on the right walk along the field edge with a hedgerow on your left. Now you have the biggest views, sharply right back to the tall city centre, also Emley Moor TV mast backed by a distant Pennine skyline. Swing around the field corner and down the far side to a corner stile, and then go left along the hedge side to a stile part way along. This sends a short enclosed path up onto an old road, The Avenue.

3. To your right it bridges the motorway, but your way is left, rapidly improving into a delightful enclosed green way almost sandwiched between the audible motorway and estate woodland. At a bend it swings left and becomes surfaced to approach Bullerthorpe Lane. Don't join immediately, but merge a little further just short of the start of The Avenue on the left. This immediately reveals the mansion straight ahead. Parallel with the road, inside the grounds, is Grime's Dyke.

4. The Avenue sets a direct course for the house. Descending through Avenue Wood it drops to bridge Avenue Ponds and rises to a brow revealing the house again. As the track drops left and fades, instead drop right to find a clear path forming, slanting right down to meet a hard access road. Pass through the gap opposite, from where a path climbs beneath beeches, absorbing another path to rise to the Little Temple.

5. Resume along the firmer path that drops slowly through rhododendrons, ignoring any lesser branches right. Glimpsing a lake to your left as you meet a level path,

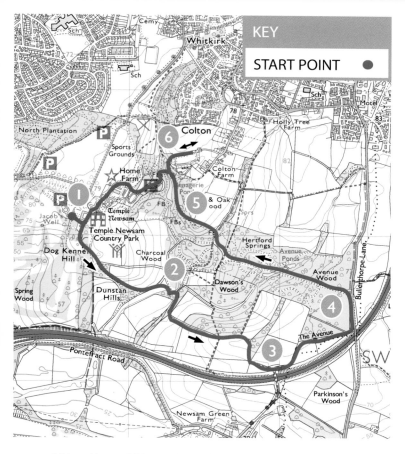

KEY

START POINT ●

go right on this to quickly reveal more of the lake. The path runs on to a junction towards the end, where you drop left onto green spaces along the lakeshore. Though your onward route is over the wooden footbridge just ahead, a very short detour advances a little further before going right up steps onto an access road with WCs to your left. Through the gates in front is the Walled Garden.

6.   Back at the footbridge, cross and bear left on the broad tarmac path, which swings away from the lake and rises alongside a hedge up the side of parkland, then climbing between rhododendrons to a path junction with the house just ahead. Turn right through large gates on a broad, cobbled way through the farm park, emerging at a car park at the end. From here rise left of the children's play area and up above the farm onto a spacious grassy area and go left towards the house to finish. Just short of it you pass the attractions of the Stable Yard.

TONG

THE LIVELY BECKS OF TWO CONVERGING WOODED VALLEYS
ARE SANDWICHED BETWEEN TWO DELIGHTFUL FORMER
PACKHORSE ROUTES DESCENDING OUT OF THE APPEALING
STREET VILLAGE OF TONG. ALL THIS IS A SURPRISING GREEN
OASIS BETWEEN TWO MAJOR NORTHERN CITIES.

Tong is a picturesque village on a lofty ridge in the centre of an extensive rural setting, yet with neither Bradford nor Leeds far away. St James' Church of 1727 has stocks outside, while set back close by is the unusually brick-built Tong Hall of 1702. The popular Greyhound pub stands by a cricket pitch among a rich assortment of characterful old houses. The Manor House dates from the 17th century. An attractive corner features a pinfold, pump and former smithy. At the end of the walk you conveniently pass Goodall's ice cream establishment, which also offers morning coffee and afternoon teas.

The neighbourhood of Tong is criss-crossed by a network of old packhorse routes by which traders – or 'jaggers' – would lead their trains of horses laden with all manner of goods from town to town and farm to farm. Both Keeper Lane and Springfield Lane display surviving sections of stone causeway – or causey – which would provide a firm footing for their ponies.

Immediately above the walk at Pudsey Beck is the 18th-century Moravian settlement at Fulneck, on the edge of the busy town of Pudsey. It was established in 1744 by a community from Moravia, in what is now the Czech Republic. It includes a splendid chapel and school among many fine old buildings and cottages, as well as a small museum and craft shop. The village overlooks the very peaceful setting of the rural valley of Pudsey Beck.

The Pudsey Beck valley is within the West Leeds Country Park, and you pass a former mill close by the beck well before reaching the more substantial Union Bridge Mills, now converted to offices with new apartments alongside.

THE BASICS

Distance: 3¼ miles / 5km

Gradient: One sustained but gentle uphill at the end

Severity: Easy walking

Approx time to walk: 2 to 2½ hrs

Stiles: Seven

Maps: OS Landranger 104 (Leeds & Bradford); Explorer 288 (Bradford & Huddersfield)

Path description: Streamside paths and old packhorse tracks

Start point: Tong village centre (GR SE 221305)

Parking: Roadside parking (BD4 0RP)

Dog friendly: Dogs preferably on leads

Public toilets: None

Nearest food: Pub at start

TONG WALK

1. From the village centre leave by heading north along Keeper Lane: this is east of the pub, marked by the pinfold and former pump. This rises away past the Manor House and ends where an enclosed way takes over at a gate. This gives a big view west as far as the wind farm on distant Ovenden Moor above Halifax before delving into greenery. Here you commence a sustained descent to the valley bottom, most of the way accompanied by the line of a stone causeway. This glorious descent takes you all the way down to a footbridge, ford and stepping stones on Pudsey Beck.

2. Across the footbridge is a junction of ways: turn right on a path running between a golf course and the wooded beck. At the end you leave by a stile, and the course is set for a delightful,

uncomplicated walk along the valley floor, always with the meandering stream close by on your right. South Park Mill is soon passed up to your left as the path remains tightly by the stream, but for the most part it is along the foot of sloping green pastures that could be anywhere. Towards the end you become enclosed by the beck again to emerge via a snicket onto a wide road, Roker Lane.

3. Drop right on the footway alongside Union Bridge Mill to a T-junction, and cross straight over to a path heading through an old gateway into trees. Don't rush off, however, but immediately leave the rising bridleway in favour of a broad path branching right. This runs a super course upstream with Tong Beck through Cockers Dale. A branch right at one stage proves to be just a muddy loop: remain on the main path until just beyond a wooden bridge over a usually dry side stream. On your right a footbridge crosses the beck at a path crossroads.

4. Across the footbridge a path ascends the other bank briefly to emerge into a field corner. It then runs left along the field bottom above the trees, and on further to enter scattered trees and undergrowth. A gate at the end returns you to the closer company of the beck. A wooden farm bridge and adjacent cattle ford are passed and on to another small gate ahead. Ignore a small footbridge on the beck, and a

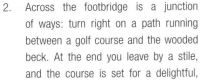

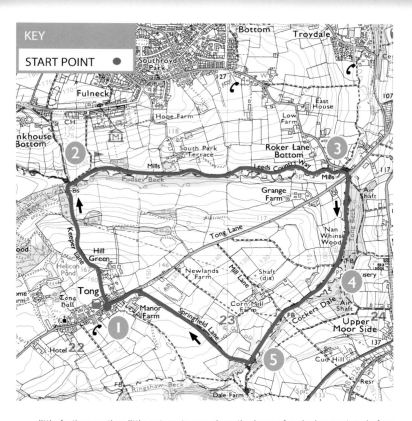

KEY

START POINT ●

little further another little gate puts you along the base of a sloping pasture before a kissing gate back into trees. After an immediate ox-bow, a long, scrubby pasture precedes arrival at an arched bridleway bridge on a kink of the beck.

5. Don't cross the bridge but turn right up the hollowed way of Springfield Lane, which commences a long climb back out of the valley. Though unbroken, it is at an easier gradient than your corresponding descent at the start of the walk. Again sections of causey are encountered on this part-hollowed way, which eases out to reveal Tong ahead. It becomes a cart track in its uppermost stages to re-enter the village street at its eastern end.

CALVERLEY BRIDGE

NEAR-LEVEL WALKING LINKS TWO VERY DIFFERENT WATERWAYS IN AN UNSUNG CORNER OF THE AIRE VALLEY. HERE THE RIVER AIRE AND LEEDS–LIVERPOOL CANAL LEAD THROUGH VERY OPEN AND RICHLY WOODED COUNTRYSIDE BETWEEN LEEDS AND BRADFORD.

Calverley is a very independent village between Leeds and Bradford, on a knoll high above bends of the river and canal, with Calverley Wood falling to the latter. St Wilfrid's Church with its 14th-century tower has a fine setting alongside the elegant Church House, a rare 18th-century semi-detached arrangement. Calverley Old Hall is a splendid old Manor House dating from the 15th century, with a medieval hall and chapel. The Calverley family lived here for centuries, before it was sold to the Thornhills in the 1750s, and after becoming several dwellings it is now owned by the Landmark Trust.

Calverley Bridge crosses the Aire just short of neighbouring Rodley, happily replaced by the modern Leeds ring-road bridge downstream. Rebuilt in 1775, it was a toll bridge until a century ago, and now makes a delightful pedestrian crossing.

Apperley Bridge sits by both the canal and the river, with popular pubs the George & Dragon and Stansfield Arms on either side of the eponymous historic bridge on the Aire. Dating from the late 18th century, its then 200-year-old predecessor had itself replaced a ford. A barely decipherable inscribed tablet adorns the bridge. A very short stroll in the opposite direction is a marina, while Dobson Locks enjoy a popular setting on the canal. Immediately on leaving Apperley Bridge the towpath passes beneath Calverley Cutting bridge. This carries the Thornhill family's Calverley Cutting of 1856, which replaced an old packhorse track through the extensive Calverley Woods.

The Leeds–Liverpool Canal runs a 127-mile (204km) course between its two great city termini, and is the northernmost of three trans-Pennine waterways. The canal engineers took advantage of the low-level Aire Gap to breach the Pennines by way of a chain of locks, only resorting to tunnelling for a mile-long stretch at its summit at Foulridge on the Lancashire border. Begun in 1770 and fully opened in 1816 for what proved to be a short-lived industrial use, it was swiftly overtaken by the arrival of the railways. Today it is a vibrant leisure amenity, for walkers, bargees, anglers, naturalists, and, in places, cyclists.

THE BASICS

Distance: 4¾ miles / 7.5km

Gradient: Negligible

Severity: Very easy

Approx time to walk: 2½ to 3 hrs

Stiles: Two

Maps: OS Landranger 104 (Leeds & Bradford); Explorer 288 (Bradford & Huddersfield)

Path description: Mostly towpath and riverbank walking

Start point: Calverley Bridge (GR SE 221368)

Parking: Canalside parking area just beneath modern ring-road bridge off A6120 (LS13 1PY)

Dog friendly: Dogs preferably on leads

Public toilets: None

Nearest food: Pub and refreshments at start, pubs and café at Apperley Bridge

CALVERLEY BRIDGE WALK

1. Saving the canal towpath for the return leg, begin by bearing right, slowly away from the towpath along a rough road past a few houses leading to the Railway pub. Continue past it down an old road to reach the 'real' Calverley Bridge. Across, advance a few steps to a path crossroads, then turn left on a few steps down into a riverside pasture. Head away upstream beneath an enormous pylon, with a large factory over to the right. The tapering field puts you more firmly on a better riverbank path at the end, noting the big, circular red-brick chimney at Woodbottom. The path passes through an arched tunnel beneath double railway bridges and pleasantly on for some time until deflected away from the river.

2. When the path is deflected from the river by a wall to meet a broader path, go left on this wall-side way beneath a large field. Broadening, it emerges at a surfaced waterworks road end by a lone house. Drop left a few strides and along outside the garden's bottom edge to a simple footbridge into a field. A firm path heads off along the foot of Cragg Wood, soon arriving back on the riverbank.

3. A delightful section is now enjoyed, opening out with nice views on the right and wonderful river scenery. Further, the path passes beneath Woodhouse Bridge, a railway viaduct, and then on past sports fields. Towards the end the official path turns sharp right, enclosed, to meet a driveway going left out onto the A658 at Apperley Bridge.

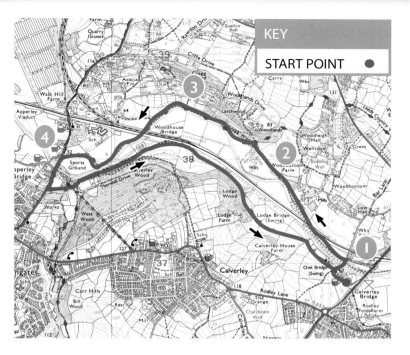

KEY

START POINT ●

4.   The main route turns left over the modern road bridge. To visit the actual bridge or the pubs either side of it you must cross the main road, there going left on the old road crossing Apperley Bridge. Across, turn left past the George & Dragon back to the main road, using pedestrian lights to cross. Ignoring Parkin Lane, turn right, rising briefly to canal bridge 214A where you drop left down steps to gain the towpath. Head away to the left and almost immediately walk beneath the Calverley Cutting bridge. After a farm on the left and a string of moored barges on the right, the towpath leads grandly on with much woodland and later open pastures across the water. Initially, too, the Aire itself also provides company, and a canal milestone is passed. Ultimately you will end up back at your starting point.

SALTAIRE

Two colourful waterways lead to beautiful woodland and gritstone outcrops at a classic Yorkshire landmark, all starting and ending at a World Heritage Site from the era of Victorian industrial pomp.

Saltaire was created as a mill village by Sir Titus Salt, who moved his workers to this greenfield site from the polluted air and slums of Bradford. From 1850 to 1872 hundreds of terraced stone dwellings were built to house the workforce of his new worsted processing mill. This outstanding piece of industrial architecture, 550 feet (170m) long and six storeys high, is a sight to behold. The village's grid-iron system remains virtually intact, along with the schools, almshouses, hospital and institute that followed. Salt's notable omission – since rectified – was a public house. Most buildings function as originally intended, and this major conservation area was designated a World Heritage Site in 2001.

Local entrepreneur Jonathan Silver bought Salts Mill in 1987 and transformed it to support myriad uses, and pride of place goes to the exhibitions of work by celebrated Bradford-born artist David Hockney. Aside from the mill itself, the finest of Salt's buildings is the Congregational Church (now the United Reformed Church), built in 1859 in rich Italian style, with a semicircular front and ornate circular tower. Across the river is Roberts Park, a tribute to Salt's work and an important amenity for his millworkers: a statue of Salt was erected in 1903 on his birth centenary. The Leeds–Liverpool Canal has flowed through the area since long before Saltaire existed, and the towpath continues out to Hirst Wood, with its lock and aqueduct on the river. Each September the Saltaire Festival proves a vibrant, cultural extravaganza.

Shipley Glen has been a place of public resort since Victorian townsfolk first escaped urban grime for weekend fresh air. A lengthy escarpment of gritstone crags and boulders fringes the edge of the linear common, overlooking the deep wooded valley of Loadpit Beck. The roadside Bracken Hall is a countryside centre with exhibitions and displays on local history and wildlife. Just outside it is part of a Bronze Age circle known as the Soldiers' Trench, with at least 60 stones still in place.

Your return to the valley is alongside a remarkable survivor, the Shipley Glen Cable Tramway: built in 1895, its open cars convey visitors up and down the wooded bank to the glen. Until quite recently the remaining parts of Shipley Glen Pleasure Grounds stood on Prod Lane, with a small funfair for children; a century ago visitors were thrilled by what were then exhilarating rides, joined in the 1930s by an aerial glide that was only finally dismantled in the 21st century.

THE BASICS

Distance: 4½ miles / 7.2km

Gradient: One steady rise to the edge of Shipley Glen

Severity: Largely undemanding

Approx time to walk: 2½ to 3 hrs

Stiles: None

Maps: OS Landranger 104 (Leeds & Bradford); Explorer 288 (Bradford & Huddersfield)

Path description: Towpath and good woodland and moorland paths

Start point: Saltaire railway station (GR SE 139380)

Parking: Car park and roadside parking (BD18 4PP)

Dog friendly: Dogs preferably on leads

Public toilets: At start and Shipley Glen

Nearest food: Pubs and cafes at start, pub/café on Shipley Glen

SALTAIRE WALK

1. From the station turn down Victoria Road, passing the Congregational Church and bridging the Leeds–Liverpool Canal. Turn left to join and follow the towpath away from the village. Beyond Hirst Wood Lock, the greenery of Hirst Wood makes for a lovely stroll to an aqueduct over the River Aire, which has been parallel for some time.

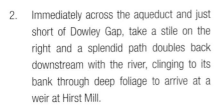

2. Immediately across the aqueduct and just short of Dowley Gap, take a stile on the right and a splendid path doubles back downstream with the river, clinging to its bank through deep foliage to arrive at a weir at Hirst Mill.

3. Here you leave the river on the driveway rising up to a T-junction with an old carriageway. Go left on a gentle slant between hedgerows up to a lodge. Here go right up a continuing rougher enclosed track that ascends to an old iron kissing gate onto a bridle-track with a cobbled central strip. Engulfed in woodland rise left on this, emerging at the top where it broadens and loses the cobbled surface.

4. At this point take a stile on the right and up the side of a paddock to an old house on the edge of Gilstead. Bear right between garages to a small iron gate back into woodland, and just a few strides further a broad path is met. Now on the edge of Shipley Glen, turn left and stay on this grand path through oak woodland high above Loadpit Beck. Ultimately as the ravine becomes shallower the path forks; as the left branch rises to join Lode Pit Lane on the edge of Eldwick, your way slants down to a stone-arched bridge on the beck.

5. Cross the bridge marking the walk's turning point and follow the main path doubling back right up the heathery bank, now on the open country of Shipley Glen proper. Continue across the open grass, along the crest of a broken gritstone edge that forms above the wooded bank. With the road only a short distance to the left, this option avoids motor but not human traffic as it leads along the full length of the glen. Remain on open ground all the way to the Old Glen House pub and tearooms at the far end.

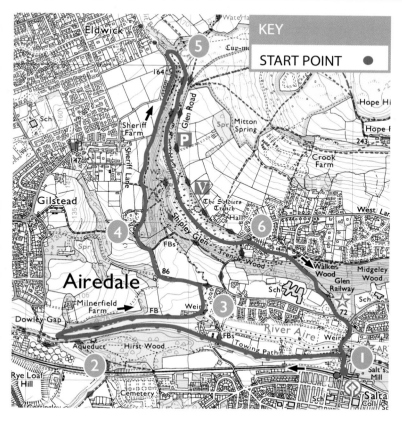

KEY

START POINT   ●

6. From the end of the open country at the Old Glen House, continue along suburban Prod Lane to the top station of the Shipley Glen Cable Tramway. To its right a surfaced path descends Trench Wood to the bottom station, and runs on to join Higher Coach Road. Virtually opposite is an entrance to Roberts Park, which is worthy of exploration despite the quickest finish being to go left around its edge to a large metal footbridge on the Aire. The start of the walk is just up above.

BINGLEY

TOWPATH AND BECK-SIDE WALKING LEADS TO A LOVELY OLD VILLAGE, THOUGH THE WALK'S HIGHLIGHT IS THE IMPRESSIVE FIVE RISE LOCKS ON THE LEEDS-LIVERPOOL CANAL, ABLY SUPPORTED BY ITS UNDERLING THE THREE RISE LOCKS.

Bingley is a bustling town which retains some older corners, notably the lovely environs of All Saints' Church with its solid 15th-century tower. Across the road the Old White Horse Inn dates from the 17th century, alongside the similarly aged Ireland Bridge on the Aire. In spacious Myrtle Park is the Georgian Town Hall, formerly the Busfield family's Myrtle Grove with coach house and stables. The park makes a green buffer between the main street and the river; indeed a remarkable aspect of the town is that the Aire's parallel course has repelled development on its western bank. The park also hosts two popular annual events, the long-established Bingley Show and an increasingly ambitious popular music festival.

Centrally placed is the splendid open market hall of 1693, alongside a covered Buttercross of possibly 13th-century origin, and the restored 18th-century stocks. The Leeds–Liverpool Canal flows through the heart of town, and was re-aligned to accommodate the 21st-century bypass, which contrary to tradition goes plum through the centre of town!

The Five Rise Locks are a major landmark of the Leeds–Liverpool Canal. For over 200 years, five interlinking locks have lifted boats up this watery staircase – a fascinating spectacle and a fine piece of engineering. This is a hugely popular location, with the lock-keeper's house – a lock-keeper still oversees this busy scene – and a café at the top. The Three Rise Locks perform a similar if inevitably less exciting role in the shadow of the landmark Damart factory.

Named from the Norse for 'big clearing', Micklethwaite is an enviably sited little village awash with characterful dwellings. A steeply sloping upper green sends the road winding down through the village. Attractive groupings include High Fold opposite the Methodist chapel of 1875.

Further down the main street is Micklethwaite Grange, dating from 1695. Legend suggests that Oliver Cromwell fired on the original grange with cannon positioned on the Druid's Altar across the valley. The lower green features a maypole, watched over by the hugely attractive Manor House of 1601. Concealed by Morton Beck, Holroyd Mill of 1812 retains its chimney and millpond.

THE BASICS

Distance: 3¾ miles / 6km

Gradient: One notable rise from the canal to the top of Micklethwaite

Severity: Easy to moderate

Approx time to walk: 2½ hrs

Stiles: Seven

Maps: OS Landranger 104 (Leeds & Bradford); Explorer 288 (Bradford & Huddersfield)

Path description: Canal towpath, assorted field paths and a snicket

Start point: Bingley railway station (GR SE 107391)

Parking: Central car parks (BD16 2LZ)

Dog friendly: Dogs preferably on leads

Public toilets: At start

Nearest food: Pubs and cafes at start, café at Five Rise Locks, pub at Crossflatts

BINGLEY WALK

1. From the station turn right onto Park Road, and then right again as it bridges the dual carriageway. After crossing the parallel Leeds–Liverpool Canal take a path left down onto its bank, and head away past the Damart factory to reach the Three Rise Locks. Cross by a swing bridge at the top and resume on the towpath, quickly revealing the Five Rise Locks ahead. Ascend alongside the locks to the top, a popular location with its cafe and lock-keeper's house.

2. Saving possible refreshment for when you return to this point, for now simply advance on the towpath past colourful boats to soon arrive at Micklethwaite Wharf. Cross Micklethwaite Lane and continue along the towpath above Crossflatts to a swing bridge on Morton Lane, where you abandon the canal, for now.

3. Cross the bridge and almost at once take a gap-stile on the right. From it a surfaced path heads away to shortly enter a few trees. Here take a right fork to cross a footbridge on Morton Beck, and resume upstream. A stile into a field takes you outside the beck up to a stile onto a level path. Go left; rejoining the beck to soon reach a delectable, tree-fringed millpond, with the old chimney still evident across it. Resuming, the mill-cut is bridged and the beck leads to a stile alongside a bridge on it. Don't cross this, but instead turn right on the enclosed ascending way, an improving course which runs on to merge into an access road to enter a corner of Micklethwaite. Remain on this access road as it winds left through a cluster of housing. Turning right at the end it rises onto the road through the village alongside a chapel and opposite High Fold.

4. Go left a few strides to a steep, sloping green, whose 'summit' seats may well delay you. Leave by the hairpin bend on the right, where a level path heads away from a gate/stile to another gate/stile across the field. Through this a drive is joined to lead on beneath a heather bank and above Fair Lady Farm to a stile at the end. A grand path heads away, soon becoming enclosed by walls to run a delightful, largely level course with views right to the Druid's Altar far across the valley, and scattered bracken woodland above. At the end your path emerges onto steeply climbing Greenhill Lane. Turn left up its footway to a junction at the top with Lady Lane.

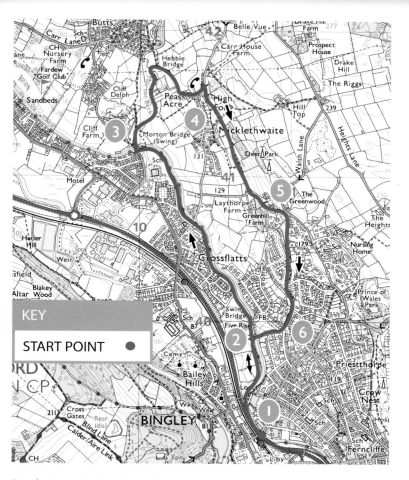

KEY

START POINT ●

5. On the very junction take a bridle-gate on the right, and a firm path winds down through a sliver of woodland. This course is maintained for some time, remarkably so amid much encroaching suburbia. Ultimately it drops onto a street. Cross to Pinedale and descend to find a corner snicket to the left sending you off again. Through further greenery this drops to a narrow access road. Look to the right to see the late 16th-century house of Gawthorpe Hall tucked away with some old cottages close by. From a stile and steps opposite descend to a kissing gate onto a driveway which leads down onto a through road. Turn right above some allotments, and at the end go left down Beck Lane to return to the top of the Five Rose Locks.

6. Across the bridge turn left on the towpath to retrace your opening steps back into Bingley.

ILKLEY

INVIGORATING STRIDES LEAD ACROSS THE INCOMPARABLE LANDSCAPES OF WORLD-FAMOUS ILKLEY MOOR, KNOWN BY MANY ONLY IN SONG AS THE YORKSHIRE ANTHEM GOES 'ON ILKLA MOOR BAHT'AT'. BETTER TO KNOW IT IN PERSON, ON THIS WALK CONNECTING A HOST OF LANDMARKS FROM THE CELEBRATED COW & CALF ROCKS TO THE ENIGMATIC SWASTIKA STONE.

Ilkley is the highest town on the River Wharfe, a perfect stepping stone between industrial conurbations downstream and the Yorkshire Dales immediately upstream. This thriving town blends a workaday existence with that of a tourist venue, as shops, pubs and cafes line spacious streets decorated by floral colour. All Saints' Church has a 500-year-old tower and Anglo-Saxon crosses, and also covers part of the site of a Roman fort. Also by the church is the 16th-century Manor House Museum. Originally serving the packhorse trade, the shapely Old Bridge was rebuilt after the great flood of 1673 that swept away many of the Wharfe's bridges.

Once known as the Hanging Stones, the Cow & Calf Rocks are one of Yorkshire's premier landmarks. This is a very popular climbing area, though the Cow's buttress is so uncompromising that most climbers will be found in the quarry round the back. Below the Cow is its offspring the Calf, whose scooped steps offer an angled scramble. A refreshment kiosk is supplemented by the roadside Cow & Calf Hotel.

The humble cottage of White Wells is a monument to Ilkley's early spa days. In the 18th century Squire Middleton long pre-empted the Victorians by building White Wells as a bath-house to enable townsfolk to enjoy a dip in pure moorland spring water. It is now a visitor centre with refreshments. Inside, a deep circular pool is hollowed from the rock and fed by a cold mineral spring – you can still normally take a plunge if you bring your gear.

Ilkley flourished as a spa town and the Victorians revelled in the healing powers of its waters. By the turn of the 19th century the fashion had passed, but by then Ilkley was firmly on the tourist map. Passed just before the end, Wells House was built in 1856 as one of a number of hydropath establishments catering for the demand for curing ailments by means of liberal contact with the cold waters that sprang from the moor. It later served as a college and is now luxury apartments.

High on Woodhouse Crag, the Swastika Stone is thought to date from Bronze Age times, sharing the characteristics of symbols found in Scandinavia and elsewhere. The main carving visible is a replica, the original being less discernible on the main rock further back.

THE BASICS

Distance: 4¾ miles / 7.6km

Gradient: One short rise near the start

Severity: Moderate

Approx time to walk: 3 hrs

Stiles: None

Maps: OS Landranger 104 (Leeds & Bradford); Explorer 297 (Lower Wharfedale & Washburn Valley)

Path description: Moorland paths, mostly good and firm

Start point: Darwin Gardens at top of Wells Road (GR SE 117471)

Parking: Car park at Darwin Gardens (LS29 9TF)

Dog friendly: Sheep grazing on the moor, dogs preferably on leads

Public toilets: Town centre, White Wells

Nearest food: Pubs and cafes in the town

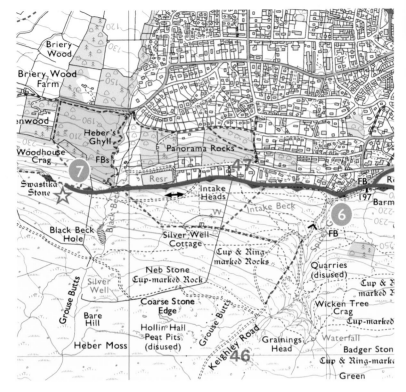

1. From a gate left of the cattle grid follow a surfaced driveway rising left up the moor. This soon slims into a surfaced path rising through bracken to arrive at The Tarn, an artificial but attractive scene. At its far end a few steps send a path off, rising gently to meet one from the right to reach a footbridge on deeply-incised Backstone Beck.

2. Across the beck, take the left option which rises steadily, then runs on through bracken: approaching a plantation keep left at a fork, easing out beneath rock outcrops beyond. Crossing a green quarry track keep right to suddenly arrive at the Calf, with the Cow up to your right.

3. A flagged path rises between them to a quarry entrance between the cliffs. Drop briefly left to

KEY

START POINT ●

a flagged path rising to the far end of the rocks, and — being aware of substantial drops — surmount the higher rocks to appraise a wonderful scene with views to match. From the top the higher crest of Ilkley Crags is prominent back across the moor. Strike out in this direction on a path going right from a junction just down to your left, crossing a patch of heather then on to arrive at the higher reaches of Backstone Beck.

4. Across the beck, drop a short way to the lower path rising away. This runs beneath Ilkley Crags into Rocky Valley, and grandly on below scattered outcrops to emerge at the end with more big views over Ilkley Moor. The path runs on to meet a broader one descending from the end of Ilkley Crags, and this goes down to the cottage at White Wells.

5. Head away from White Wells down its broad access track. After a stream crossing go left on a wide, level path. This runs a good course through bracken, narrowing but avoiding any lesser branches to lead unfailingly to Keighley Road.

6. Go left a few strides to bridge Spicey Gill, and then from a small parking area just beyond it, a firm path bears right across the foot of the moor. It leads to a broad path just above the wall, which rises steadily along the moor-foot. Ignoring other paths, remain on this, passing Panorama Reservoir over the wall to reach a footbridge on Black Beck above the woods of Heber's Ghyll. Emerging from the stream's confines just beyond at a corner gate, slant left up to a firm, higher path, and turn briefly right along it to reach the Swastika Stone, guarded by iron railings on the escarpment of Woodhouse Crag.

7. Retrace your steps on this broad path, and this time remain on it as it later swings back to meet your previous path beyond Panorama Reservoir. Retrace your steps to Keighley Road at the bridge on Spicey Gill, and simply turn left on this, which drops right to a junction. Keep right on this now broad road which runs unfailingly along the foot of the moor to return to your start point.

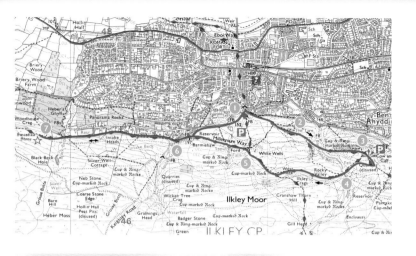

OTLEY CHEVIN

BIG VIEWS AND EASY WALKING PREDOMINATE IN THIS RAMBLE
WITHIN THE POPULAR CHEVIN FOREST PARK. IN THE CARE
OF LEEDS CITY COUNCIL, THE PARK IS SPLIT BETWEEN OTLEY
CHEVIN TO THE WEST AND DANEFIELD TO THE EAST.

The Chevin is Otley's answer to Zermatt's Matterhorn, a tall upland ridge that hovers faithfully over its town. The walk's starting point is also virtually its summit, and offers expansive views over the Wharfe Valley from a rewarding mix of woodland and moorland, including a bird's-eye view of Otley itself. Other features will be better identified at the end of the walk. The name Chevin is derived from the Celtic cefn, meaning ridge or back, and the road along the crest is York Gate, itself an ancient route.

All the land on the east side of East Chevin Road was the Danefield estate and Caley Deer Park of nearby Farnley Hall. It was presented to the town in 1946 by Major Horton-Fawkes as a memorial to its war dead. Today it offers a rich selection of footpath and bridleway routes. The rock-climbing ground of Caley Crags is a fine place to linger as the gritstone edge offers sweeping Wharfedale views. Down below is Pool's busy bridge over the Wharfe, backed by the rocky boss of Almscliff Crag across the valley.

The White House is a Chevin institution, based within an old farmhouse that has offered refreshments to visitors since Victorian times. Purchased by Leeds City Council in 1977, it has a café, information and WCs, and is normally open from 11am to 2pm, daily except Tuesdays, and until 3pm at weekends. Beacon Hill Moor forms the steep slopes between the beacon and the dense woods below. The return path along its base shadows an uncommonly seen vaccary wall, whose particularly thick slabs kept cattle corralled within its confines.

At the end of the walk you can enjoy a final panorama aided by the presence of a rangefinder on the Beacon House site. This picks out such varied man-made creations as Emley Moor and Holme Moss masts, York Minster, Arthington Viaduct, Kilburn White

Horse and Ferrybridge power station. Distant natural features include Great Whernside in the Yorkshire Dales and Boulsworth Hill on the Lancashire border. Nearer to hand, across the Wharfe, are Farnley Hall, Denton and Middleton Moors and Beamsley Beacon.

The Beacon House, known as Jenny's Cottage after a former occupant, was fully demolished in 1976. This has been the setting for many a fire, to warn of approaching danger or more usually to celebrate happy, invariably royal, events. It is also the location of a 30-foot-high wooden cross, erected annually to mark the start of Holy Week leading up to Easter, and clearly visible to townsfolk in the streets below.

THE BASICS

Distance: 4¼ miles / 6.8km

Gradient: Mostly undulating, one steep rise near the end

Severity: Moderate

Approx time to walk: 2½ to 3 hrs

Stiles: None

Maps: OS Landranger 104 (Leeds & Bradford); Explorer 297 (Lower Wharfedale & Washburn Valley)

Path description: Well-used paths through woodland and moorland

Start point: Surprise View on York Gate, just west of Royalty pub (GR SE 204440)

Parking: Car park at Surprise View on York Gate (LS20 9NP)

Dog friendly: Dogs preferably on leads

Public toilets: White House

Nearest food: Tearooms (not Mondays) above Shawfield, White House café (not Tuesdays)

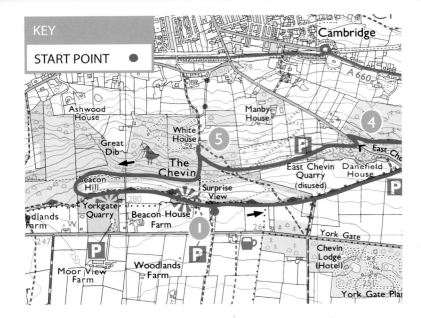

1. At the end of the car park you emerge immediately onto Surprise View on the crest of the Chevin. A broad path runs right along the top of Beacon Hill Moor, ignoring branches before dropping to join Miller Lane. Head along this gently declining, enclosed track to reach East Chevin Road. Cross to a broad path into the woods of Danefield, rising right to Lower Shawfield car park.

2. Just yards to your left is a major fork: head away on the main track, Chippendale Ride (named after Otley's famous cabinet-maker son), into the plantations. Rising to a junction beyond a tiny beck, keep straight on. This broad way runs a straight, near-level course through the trees, later absorbing a branch from below before reaching the end of the trees at a path junction. Turn left through a kissing-gate and immediately fork right. A path curves down through open country to the crest of the lower grouping of Caley Crags.

3. Resume left on the crest: in deeper trees a kissing-gate puts you onto a broader

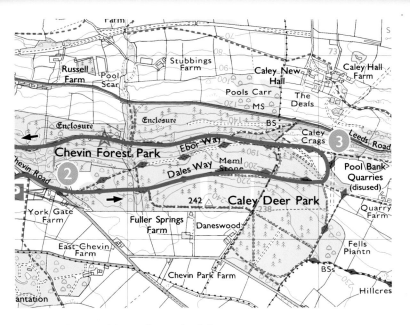

track; keep straight on. At a major fork take the lower track slanting down to a junction, just past which it enters further massive boulders of Caley Crags. Beyond these the path drops steadily down and along to a junction just before crossing a stone bridge. This continues as a broad carriageway back onto East Chevin Road at Danefield Gate. Turn briefly up the footway and cross to East Chevin Quarry car park.

4. A broad path rises away to run beneath quarried cliffs, easing out before moorland slopes are revealed below. Further on, woodland is re-entered and the path meets a broad track descending from the foot of Beacon Hill Moor. Turn uphill for a direct return, but for the full route bear right down the track, deeper into woodland to reach a crossroads with a steeply descending

path. Just 100 paces further is the White House.

5. Retrace steps to the crossroads where more than 200 steps offer a direct ascent to the foot of Beacon Hill Moor, going straight up to the waiting rocks on the Beacon site. However, for further pleasures turn right on a broad path along the top of White House Plantation, shadowed by the slabs of a vaccary wall. These abruptly end, but the path and trees remain. Some seventy strides beyond a broad path junction turn up a thin path immediately after an old wall. This rises through dense bilberry bushes to join a higher-level path, and doubling back along it past the Chevin's anonymous highest point the rocks are quickly gained.

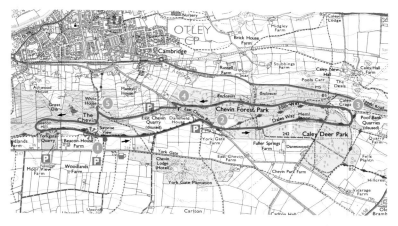

HAREWOOD

A BEAUTIFUL AND EASY WALK THROUGH ELEGANT
PARKLAND. WHILE GLIMPSES OF ONE OF YORKSHIRE'S GREAT
STATELY HOMES ARE GUARANTEED, RATHER MORE MOVEABLE
BUT NEVERTHELESS LIKELY ARE SIGHTINGS OF RED AND
FALLOW DEER AND RED KITES.

Immediately outside the entrance to Harewood House, the estate village of Harewood perches high above the Wharfe's final hilly miles. Several weekends throughout the year see these slopes host colourful hill climbs, when all manner of sporty machines spiral their way up from the Wharfe meadows. The Harewood Arms stands among neat dwellings, as does a village shop. A short concessionary path is signed off a public path through a tiny housing estate just north of the start of the walk, and runs through the trees to the hidden but impressive remains of Harewood Castle, which dates from the mid-14th century. Harewood Bridge is a major crossing point of the Wharfe.

The redundant church of All Saints sits in a bluebell-carpeted churchyard within the estate grounds. Dating from the 15th century, it was restored in Victorian times. An old sundial sits above the porch door, while inside are some fine medieval monuments.

One of Yorkshire's premier stately homes, Harewood House is the seat of the Earl of Harewood, a title first bestowed in 1812 on Edwin Lascelles, whose family came over with William the Conqueror. Dating from 1759, Harewood House was built on profits of the Lascelles' West Indian sugar plantations. This magnificent mansion boasts a fine pedigree, being designed by John Carr of York, with interiors by Robert Adam, furniture by Thomas Chippendale, and grounds courtesy of Capability Brown. Victorian architect Sir Charles Barry was responsible for the third storey, and created an Italianate terrace along the south facade. The resplendent rooms are particularly notable for housing an extensive fine art collection alongside outstanding furnishings.

Still in the hands of the same family, the house and grounds are open to the fee-paying public and are a very popular draw. Within the grounds is a long-established bird garden, while numerous special interest events take place throughout the year. Woodland and lakeside walks lead through delightful surrounds, and the herds of deer that roam the grounds are almost certain to be encountered. A more recent development has been the hugely successful release of previously endangered red kites, and these magnificent birds of prey are now a regular sight soaring above the grounds.

THE BASICS

Distance: 5 miles / 8km

Gradient: One steady rise through parkland

Severity: Easy

Approx time to walk: 3 hrs

Stiles: None

Maps: OS Landranger 104 (Leeds & Bradford); Explorer 289 (Leeds) or 297 (Lower Wharfedale & Washburn Valley)

Path description: Mostly firm estate tracks, and a woodland path

Start point: Harewood village centre (GR SE 321451)

Parking: Village hall car park on Church Lane (LS17 9LQ)

Dog friendly: Dogs preferably on leads, and must be on leads in Wall Side Plantation

Public toilets: None

Nearest food: Pub and village shop at start

HAREWOOD WALK

1. From the main entrance gates at the traffic lights, head north on the footway and turn left on Church Lane to the village hall, if you're not indeed already there. Just past the hall keep straight on a private road, passing right of a neat lodge. This runs on between woods to emerge into the open. Ahead is a grand prospect across the  Wharfe Valley to the landmarks of Norwood Edge and Almscliff Crag. A short detour from this point goes left on a walled track to enter the churchyard.

2. Back on the access road, resume along the brow. Bigger views ahead reveal Otley Chevin, and Rombalds Moor beyond the arches of Wharfedale Viaduct; Kirkby Overblow sits on the skyline back to the right, with the busy junction at Harewood Bridge just below. The road drops to a crossroads of bridleways; keep left on the main one which swings along an open pasture to the environs of Harewood Yard at Stank. This complex was the site of Home Farm, abandoned in the 1980s in favour of a tasteful conversion to offices.

3. Advance straight on, through a gate and down another access road to cross Stank Beck. Keep straight on, joining another road from the left and rising steeply past a lone house. A little further, bear right at a fork past a tall red-brick wall, past which keep right again at another fork through a belt of trees. This rises outside Carr Wood to Carr House. Before continuing, look back for the first glimpse of Harewood House and its lake. Rising past the buildings a track continues up into trees, swinging right on merging with a broader track. This steady rise doubles back left onto a brow, ignoring a branch right through a gateway.

4. This level track again runs through lovely woodland. A cluster of stone buildings visible over the wall to the right is the purpose-built set of TV soap Emmerdale, keeping this one-time farming drama far from the public gaze. The track runs on to a triangular junction, where you bear left down to the graceful, stone-arched New Bridge. Turn right over this and the track quickly leaves the trees to rise in style through open parkland. This archetypal landscape soon offers views back to the house across the rolling grounds. Continuing to rise, it then runs a high, level course over the spacious Lodge Hills to approach large gates alongside a lodge. There is now a better-proportioned view of the majestic frontage of Harewood House.

5. Beyond the gates is the A61 road, but this is neatly avoided by a permissive path which remains within the grounds. This can occasionally be closed for short periods:

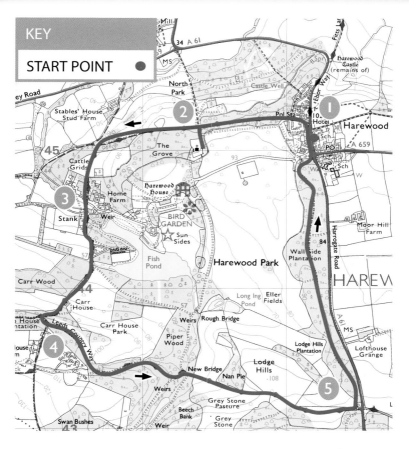

KEY

START POINT ●

in this unlikely event the only alternative is either to tramp the last mile along the road, or significantly extend the walk by using rights of way further east. Turn left in front of the lodge and commence the last leg on the Wallside Path. Dropping to a gate into Wall Side Plantation, the broad path runs a splendid course, never far from the high wall that keeps you from the invisible but audible traffic. Becoming broader, ultimately the track reaches a gate fronting a wildlife conservation area. Here a footpath is deflected right to the wall side alongside a ruin featuring a lintel dated 1675. Pass through the gate in the estate wall onto the hubbub of the road, and a footway leads left back to the start.

EAST KESWICK

THIS IS A LEISURELY RAMBLE AROUND FIELDS AND WOODS
AMONG THE WELL-HEELED COMMUTER VILLAGES NORTH-EAST
OF LEEDS. BARDSEY HAS NUMEROUS HISTORIC HIGHLIGHTS
INCLUDING ITS CHURCH, PUB AND CASTLE SITE, WHILE
GRITSTONE CRAGS AND INTRIGUING EARTHWORKS FEATURE
AROUND HETCHELL WOOD.

East Keswick is the northernmost of
a cluster of neighbouring villages that
are distant rural satellites of the Leeds
district. Its features include the church
of St Mary Magdalen and two pubs, the
Old Star and the Duke of Wellington.
An old West Riding road sign stands at
the junction outside the former smithy,
and a working clock adorns an adjacent
building.

Bardsey is a leafy village greatly extended by modern housing. Enclosed within a lovely
churchyard, All Hallows boasts a splendid Anglo-Saxon tower, with other parts dating
from Norman times. Just along the street is the Bingley Arms, one of several pubs laying
claim to be England's oldest as its origins date from AD 953. Despite being rebuilt down
the centuries, it is said the older part has survived for over a thousand years: there are
priest holes secreted in the fireplace. Located roughly halfway between Kirkstall Abbey
and York, it was possibly a place to break their journey for monks travelling between the
two places.

On Woodacre Lane stands Callister Hall with a 1726 date stone, while Bardsey Grange
was the birthplace in 1670 of Restoration dramatist William Congreve. Easily seen on the
return path into Bardsey, the grassy knoll of Castle Hill is the very well-defined site of a
Norman motte and bailey; originally timber, the late 12th-century stone castle of Adam
de Bruce had but a brief existence.

The unexpectedly colourful country of Pompocali features very distinctive earthworks that
are the residue from quarrying, with gritstone found pretty much on-site and Magnesian
limestone being won just up the hill. This intriguing landscape has Roman connections,
as their road between Ilkley and York passed through here, largely on the course of the
bridleway dividing Pompocali and Hetchell Wood.

Hetchell Wood is a nature reserve of the Yorkshire Wildlife Trust, and the impressive gritstone facade of Hetchell Crags offers climbers a choice of more than 50 named routes. Near the wood the walk twice encounters the old Leeds–Wetherby railway line, opened in 1877 and closed in 1964 as a result of the infamous Beeching cuts; all that remain are grassy embankments.

THE BASICS

Distance: 4¾ miles / 7.6km

Gradient: Two minor uphill sections

Severity: Easy walking

Approx time to walk: 3 hrs

Stiles: Three

Maps: OS Landranger 104 (Leeds & Bradford); Explorer 289 (Leeds)

Path description: Good field and woodland paths; some road walking

Start point: East Keswick village centre (GR SE 360444)

Parking: Roadside parking (LS17 9EH)

Dog friendly: Dogs preferably on leads

Public toilets: None

Nearest food: Two pubs at start, one at Bardsey

1. From the centre head south to the village edge. Just after the Duke of Wellington a path is signed left of a cottage. Across a footbridge it ascends between fields onto a road. Go left a few strides then right up the footway alongside Woodacre Lane. At the top it runs past a school and down to a T-junction in the centre of Bardsey.

2. Cross into the churchyard to find a small gate at the bottom, opposite the porch. A path drops to a footbridge, and up the other side into a field. Slanting right to the field side, it then makes a sustained pull outside modern housing. On the brow turn right onto the bend of an enclosed path, and go left on this to the head of an access road. Advance along this past the houses of Wayside Gardens onto the A58.

3. Cross and go a few strides left to find a path heading away along a field side to meet a track coming in from the left. At this point take a path rising right with a hedge. Over a brow it drops to the corner, from where a path runs left through undergrowth with a tiny stream. Further, the path crosses a footbridge to emerge into a field. Go left on the hedge side to a stile onto a driveway in front of a house. Go briefly left to the gates of Moat Hall.

4. Turn right on an enclosed path round two sides of a field, then bridging a beck and on beneath a rail bridge. The way continues for some time to a ruinous mill, just beyond which it runs through undergrowth to arrive beneath heathery mounds at Pompocali. Ascend the path straight ahead, and at an early fork keep straight on above the drop to your left. With heathery mounds to your right advance to the brow, and at the end of the hummocks is a T-junction with another path. This drops left to find a bridle-gate onto an enclosed track. Drop left to a ford and bridge, but without crossing take a kissing-gate on the right into Hetchell Wood.

5. A good path heads away with Hetchell Crags just above, and at the end you emerge into a sloping field. The path keeps to the left side, around a corner and into a second field to shortly enter trees at another corner. The clear path heads straight on through this largely wooded area, ignoring lesser branches left. Towards the end cross the old railway and down to the A58. Cross with care and turn right past the Bardsey junction, and a short way further take a surfaced path running left into suburban Cornmill Close.

6. Go uphill a few strides past the old corn mill on your right, and advance straight up a driveway to Bardsey Grange. Don't enter but go left through a small gateway, and a

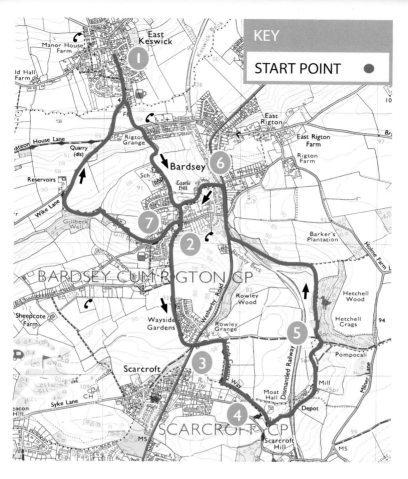

path climbs to a fence at the top enclosing Castle Hill's ancient mound. Go left with the fence, the path becoming enclosed to run past the mound and onto the road opposite the village hall.

7. For the easiest finish turn right to retrace steps to East Keswick. Otherwise, return to the T-junction by the church and turn right as far as the Bingley Arms. Opposite it a surfaced driveway heads off right with a tiny stream. At its head pass right of the right-hand gateway, and an enclosed path (not the track sharp right) heads away to emerge into a field. Advance to a stile in undergrowth, then cross the bottom edge of a sloping field above a wood. At the end, turn up the hedge side to a gate/stile onto Wike Lane. Go right to descend back into East Keswick.

ABOUT THE AUTHOR

Paul Hannon is Yorkshire born and bred, and has been writing about his native county for over thirty years. He has produced around eighty guidebooks to walks in his own and neighbouring counties Lancashire and Cumbria, as well as cycling and general guides, and has contributed to numerous magazines.

A keen photographer, he is currently making greater use of his extensive photographic archive to develop an exhaustive picture library dedicated to all things Yorkshire. Journey of the Wharfe, published in 2014, is part of an ongoing series of hardback colour titles celebrating the life and landscape of the great rivers of Yorkshire.

A father of three grown-up children, he still lives in his hometown of Keighley. When not walking and photographing, his interests include Bradford City FC, ornithology and good beer.

As a serious hill walker he has climbed hundreds of mountains in the British Isles. In 1991 he completed the 214 Lake District 'Wainwright' fells, and in 2007 became a proud Munroist on completing the 284 Scottish 3000-foot peaks on his 50th birthday.